A2 Drama Study Guide

AQA

Philip Rush

Rhinegold Education

239–241 Shaftesbury Avenue
London WC2H 8TF
Telephone: 020 7333 1720
Fax: 020 7333 1765

www.rhinegold.co.uk

Drama Study Guides
AS and A2 Drama Study Guide (Edexcel)
AS Drama Study Guide (AQA)

Music Study Guides
GCSE, AS and A2 Music Study Guides (AQA, Edexcel and OCR)
GCSE, AS and A2 Music Listening Tests (AQA, Edexcel and OCR)
GCSE Music Study Guide (WJEC)
GCSE Music Listening Tests (WJEC)
AS/A2 Music Technology Study Guide (Edexcel)
AS/A2 Music Technology Listening Test (Edexcel)
Revision Guides for GCSE (AQA, Edexcel and OCR), AS and A2 Music (AQA and Edexcel)

Also available from Rhinegold Education
Key Stage 3 Elements
Key Stage 3 Listening Tests: Book 1 and Book 2
AS and A2 Music Harmony Workbooks
GCSE and AS Music Composition Workbooks
GCSE and AS Music Literacy Workbooks
Baroque Music in Focus, Romanticism in Focus, Modernism in Focus,
Batman in Focus, *Goldfinger* in Focus, *Immaculate Collection* in Focus, *Who's Next* in Focus,
Film Music in Focus, Musicals in Focus

Rhinegold Publishing also publishes Choir & Organ, Classical Music, Classroom Music, Early Music Today, International Piano, Music Teacher, Opera Now, Piano, The Singer, Teaching Drama, British and International Music Yearbook, British Performing Arts Yearbook, British Music Education Yearbook, Rhinegold Dictionary of Music in Sound.

First published 2009 in Great Britain by
Rhinegold Publishing Limited
239–241 Shaftesbury Avenue
London WC2H 8TF
Telephone: 020 7333 1720
Fax: 020 7333 1765
www.rhinegold.co.uk

© Rhinegold Publishing Ltd 2009

All rights reserved. No part of this publication may be reproduced, stored in a retrieval system, or transmitted in any form or by any means electronic, mechanical, photocopying, recording or otherwise, without the prior permission of Rhinegold Publishing Ltd.

This title is excluded from any licence issued by the Copyright Licensing Agency, or other Reproduction Rights Organisation

Rhinegold Publishing Ltd has used its best efforts in preparing this guide. It does not assume, and hereby disclaims any liability to any party, for loss or damage caused by errors or omissions in the guide, whether such errors or omissions result from negligence, accident or other cause.

You should always check the current requirements of the examination, since these may change. Copies of the AQA Specification can be downloaded from the AQA website at www.aqa.org.uk/ or may be purchased from AQA publications, Unit Two, Wheel Forge Way, Trafford Park, Manchester M17 1EH.
Telephone: 0870 410 1036 Fax: 0161 953 1177 Email: publications@aqa.org.uk

AQA A2 Drama Study Guide (2009-2011)
British Library Cataloguing in Publication Data.
A catalogue record for this book is available from the British Library.
ISBN 978-1-906178-82-6
Printed in Great Britain by Headley Brothers Ltd

Contents

The author . . . . *page* 4

The consultant 4

Acknowledgements 4

Credit notices 4

Introduction 5
      The A2 units 5
      How to approach the course 6

Understanding Theatre 8
      What is this chapter for 8
      Practical theatre and performance terms 8
      Drama theory and analysis 15
      Understanding the text 19

Unit 3a: Pre-20th Century Texts 23
      Analysing a set text 23
      The Revenger's Tragedy 24
      Tartuffe 30
      The Recruiting Officer 38
      A Servant to Two Masters 43
      The Seagull 47
      Lady Windermere's Fan 52

Unit 3b: The 20th Century or Contemporary Drama 58
      Introduction 58
      In the exam 58
      Blood Wedding 60
      The Good Person of Szechwan 64
      A View from the Bridge 69
      The Trial 75
      Our Country's Good 79
      Coram Boy 85

Devised Drama 90
      Key features 90
      What have I got to do? 90
      Preparation and development 91
      Supporting notes 92
      Planning, researching and shaping 99
      Preparing a script 105
      Preparing a performance 111

Glossary 117

Index 118

The author

Philip Rush is the deputy head of St Peter's High School, Gloucester, where he teaches in the English department. He has taught theatre studies for 20 years and for seven years led the postgraduate training scheme for trainee English and drama teachers at the University of Gloucestershire in Cheltenham. He has a degree in English from Westfield College, University of London and an MA in drama from Bristol University. He has performed at the Edinburgh Festival Fringe and has toured with one of his own plays, which focused on the Irish famine. His poems have been published in a number of magazines including *Poetry Review* and in Carcanet's *New Poetries IV* anthology.

The consultant

John Nicol, who has been teaching English and Drama for nearly 30 years, has just been appointed Deputy Head at The Bishop of Hereford's Blue Coat School, Hereford. He is currently Arts College Director at Thorns Community College, Dudley, a specialist performing arts college. Prior to this he was Head of Performing Arts and an AST at Stourport High School, Worcestershire. The latter role involved outreach work as teacher advisor for drama in Worcestershire LEA. He has also worked as a practical moderator and written paper marker for AQA Drama.

Acknowledgements

In the writing of a guide such as this many people have contributed. The author and publishers are grateful to the following people for their specific advice, support and expert contributions: Nina Crowe, Joanna Hughes, Lucien Jenkins, Sarah Jones, Claudine Nightingale, Ben Robbins, Rose Vickridge and Sabine Wolf. The author acknowledges the input of Robert Lowe in some sections of this book. The author is also conscious of having drawn on a lifetime's reading. More recently, the growth in use of the internet has made an unparalleled amount of exciting information and challenging opinion widely available. Although every attempt has been made to acknowledge both the primary and secondary sources drawn on, it is impossible to do justice to the full range of material that has shaped the creation of this book. The author would therefore like to apologise if anyone's work has not been properly acknowledged. He would be happy to hear from authors or publishers so that any such errors or omissions may be rectified in future editions.

Credit notices

Extract from *Tartuffe* by Molière, adapted by Roger McGough (Methuen Drama, an imprint of A&C Black Publishers 2008), reprinted by permission of A&C Black Publishers.

Extract from *A Servant to Two Masters* by Carlo Osvaldo Goldoni, adapted by Lee Hall from a literal translation by Gwenda Pandolfi (Methuen Drama, an imprint of A&C Black Publishers 1999), reprinted by permission of A&C Black Publishers.

Extract from *Federico Garcia Lorca* by Reed Anderson (Macmillan 1984), reprinted by permission of Macmillan Publishers.

Extract from *The Good Person of Szechwan* by Bertolt Brecht, translated by John Willett (Methuen Drama, an imprint of A&C Black Publishers 1985), reprinted by permission of A&C Black Publishers.

Extract from *Uncle Vanya* by Anton Chekhov, translated by Michael Frayn (Methuen Drama, an imprint of A&C Black Publishers 1987), reprinted by permission of A&C Black Publishers.

Extract from Bodas de sangre/Blood Wedding by Herederos de Federico Garciá Lorca. Translation by Herederos de Federico Garciá Lorca, Michael Dewell and Carmen Zapata. All rights reserved. For information regarding rights and permissons please contact lorca@artslaw.co.uk or William Peter Kosmas Esq., 8 Franklin Square, London, W14 9UU.

Extract from *Tartuffe* by Molière, translated by Martin Sorrell (Nick Hern Books 2002), reprinted by permission of Nick Hern Books Ltd.

Introduction

Studying drama and theatre studies at A2 is naturally more challenging than it was at AS. The standard is higher and the content more demanding. What's more, you have to explore links between the various elements in order to succeed. However, it offers you exciting opportunities to build on what you have already learnt and to develop your ideas further.

During your AS course, you will have gained a wealth of experience. You will have been introduced to a range of new play texts, explored their production possibilities and considered the potential impact of these on an audience. You will have learned about playwrights and practitioners, and understood the importance of their work to the development of drama and theatre studies. You will have seen and responded to performances, created a piece of drama from a text and put together a series of notes to record each step of the creating process. All of this will have encouraged you to find new ideas and develop new skills, and you will have learned a lot about yourself and how you work with others. Building upon this base, the A2 course is an opportunity to expand your experience, knowledge and skills, and explore new play texts, practitioners and performance ideas.

Further reading

The AS companion to this book, *AQA AS Drama Study Guide* (Rhinegold 2008), will continue to be of use to you throughout the A2 course and we will refer to it frequently in this book.

The A2 units

As at AS, the A2 course consists of two units:

➢ **Unit 3:** Further Prescribed Plays including Pre-20th Century

➢ **Unit 4:** Presentation of Devised Drama.

Unit 3: Further Prescribed Plays including Pre-20th Century is worth 30% of your overall A-level mark. You will study two plays and you will be assessed on these in a two-hour written examination. There are two sections in this unit:

➢ **Section A:** Pre-20th century plays

➢ **Section B:** The 20th century or contemporary drama.

There is a choice of six plays in each of the two sections. You will study one play from each section and in the exam you will be required to answer one question on each play. For Section B, the synoptic element of the exam, a short extract from each play will be printed on the exam paper and you will be required to write about your stage realisation for this extract.

Unit 4: Presentation of Devised Drama is worth 20% of your overall A-level mark. You will work in a group towards devising a piece of drama for performance to an audience in a theatrical style of your choice. In this unit, you will be assessed by your teacher who will be moderated by an external examiner. As at AS, you will choose whether you wish to be assessed on acting, directing or design skills, and you will put together a series of supporting notes to record the process and your own contribution to it. Your mark for this unit will be based equally on the development of your work and on the presentation of your finished performance. Your notes will account for half the marks you are awarded for the development of your work.

How to approach the course

Studying a set text for A2 drama and theatre studies is not like studying a set text for an A2 English literature course. While you must understand and appreciate the text, its context, attitudes and values, you must also be able to turn this understanding and appreciation into practical ideas for performance. Although the set texts module (DRAM3) is assessed by examination essays, you will be asked to put yourself into the position of an actor, a director or a designer in order to answer the questions. The more experience you have of being a real actor, director and designer, the better.

The practical module (DRAM4), in which you put on a performance, is not entirely practical. Your acting, directing or design skills will not count for enough on their own without a theoretically informed and intellectually judged set of supporting notes which give clear details and show an understanding of your chosen theatrical style and how it relates to your devised piece.

Finding links between these practical and theoretical elements requires advanced thinking skills. While it may sound like stating the obvious, you'll have to put some proper time aside at A2 for just that: *thinking*. Only some of you will require explicit drama skills in the next stages of your life; however, you will all need to be able to think.

> Keeping your own notebook should by now be both fun and habitual. Don't be fooled into thinking that if you simply turn up to your lessons and get your work in on time, you will automatically be entitled to a top grade.

Essay writing

Essays must not be regurgitations of what has been said in lessons. Nor are they simply minutes of a discussion that has taken place. The word 'essay' derives from the French verb *essayer*, meaning 'to try out'. A good essay tries out new ideas, or new combinations of old ideas; it does not give back to the teacher what they gave to you. You should mull over questions, use your bus ride home to shape an answer and find new angles or surprising comparisons. Go back to the texts and read them through again with this new question in the front of your mind: you'll find new things to say and you'll learn more about your material. There is more to writing a good essay than memory alone.

> In the exam, put time aside for mulling over. Plan and think, then explain. Remember the key formula: describe, analyse, evaluate. This can be summed up as What? How? Why?

In an exam, the same is true. If an exam essay doesn't make you think of new combinations, new solutions and so on, alongside everything you've mastered and prepared, then you're not thinking hard enough.

So what can you do to enrich your mind?

- **See as many productions in as many theatres as possible.** Read reviews, keep an eye on the programmes of local theatres, especially small studio theatres, and discuss what you find with your teacher. When you've seen a play, make notes about it (afterwards – few things are as daft as making notes during a performance!) and think the ideas through for yourself.

- **Read plays.** You will get a more genuine understanding of genre and style if you have read as widely as possible. You can read a good play in less than an hour or so. Students who 'can't find the time' to read for themselves simply haven't looked hard enough for it.

- **Be a drama student at all times.** Watch the way people get on buses or queue for papers; watch the way men and women greet one another, the way they sit in cafes and pubs; listen to the language the people are using in the seat behind you. Anything may be relevant to your study: television programmes, new albums, clothes shops, discos, the view from a train window at night. Keep your wits about you. Actors copy; if you have nothing in your mind to copy, you'll just end up copying someone else's work.

- **Keep a diary/notebook.** Don't let your ideas blow away; jot them down. You might even want to organise a web log with other members of your group so that you can share ideas and observations, and generally take a more professional approach to the whole thing.

- **Respect your teachers.** Don't take your teachers for granted. It's a hard job and they're only doing it because they love the theatre, because they believe in the value of education and learning, and because they respect you. Help your teachers teach and they, in turn, will help you learn.

Understanding Theatre

What is this chapter for?

Each A-level subject has its own basic terminology and concepts that are unique to it. To succeed in each subject, you need to be able to understand and employ these accurately and effectively. Similarly, to understand the world of the theatre properly, there are some key ideas and terms that you must be aware of – some of which you may have already come across in your AS course, or if you regularly take part in local productions. While you will not be examined on the information in this chapter directly, your comprehension of it is integral to your success.

Some of these terms and concepts are explained more fully in later chapters, some are dealt with sufficiently here, while others could lead on to more thorough research. By using an internet search engine, you should be able to develop your enquiries.

Studying drama involves three distinct but closely related fields. Firstly, you need to know about theatres, the places dedicated to the performing of plays. You need to know how they are designed and how they work, how to describe their various features, and how lighting and scenic devices contribute to a production. In building up this knowledge you will begin to learn about the history of drama and about the different kinds of plays which make up the European theatrical tradition. Secondly, you need to know about acting – in particular, the theories that have emerged around the practice of preparing and presenting plays in performance. Finally, you need to be able to discuss play-texts subtly and professionally. For all these you will need a specialised vocabulary.

By familiarising yourself with specialist terms relating to the theatre, acting and the study of play-texts, you are establishing the foundations on which your study of theatre can be built. Reading this introduction will serve not only as a starting point to your work but also as a useful reminder as you progress, and finally as a revision aid when you face the examinations at the end of your studies.

Practical theatre and performance terms

Staging

Greek theatre

European theatre began with the ancient Greeks and we still use a lot of their terms. The history of early drama is closely linked to ancient Greek religious festivities. It is sometimes useful to think of early theatres almost as open-air temples, where the audience was like a congregation and the performance a religious ritual. The name for the place where such performances took place was *theatron*. The *skene* was the wall behind the actors which helped them to project their voices; the *orchestra* was where the 'chorus' of dancers performed. There was probably a raised stage in front of the *skene* on which the actors stood, though they could move between this and the orchestra. It is thought that Sophocles introduced the idea of painting the *skene* to give some impression of setting. The area where the audience sat was called the *koilon*.

> **Web link**
>
> For more on ancient theatres, visit http://didaskalia.open.ac.uk.

Medieval theatre

In medieval England, religious plays were performed on the feast of Corpus Christi which falls in early summer when the days are at their longest. During the day, in cities such as York and Wakefield, the guilds would perform a series of plays that enacted the main events from the history books of the Bible. The audience took up its place along a route around the town and the plays moved around during the day, so that by staying at one point, anyone could see the entire series, or cycle, of plays. These plays were performed in bright costumes and on the back of huge carts called **pageants**.

Elizabethan theatre

Secular plays, in a tradition going back to Roman times at least, were performed in public spaces, and, increasingly, in the courtyards of inns, where the audience could watch from the yard itself or could look down at the action from the corridors that ran on each storey around the yard. From this tradition the Elizabethan theatre emerged, with its characteristic **thrust stage**, bringing the actors right out into the audience, many of whom stood at their feet. Shakespeare's Globe Theatre on the south bank of the Thames in London is a modern reconstruction of such an Elizabethan theatre.

> **Web link**
>
> For more on Shakespeare's Globe, visit www.shakespeares-globe.org.

> The arrows, here as in the diagrams that follow, indicate the direction of the audience's gaze when watching the action.

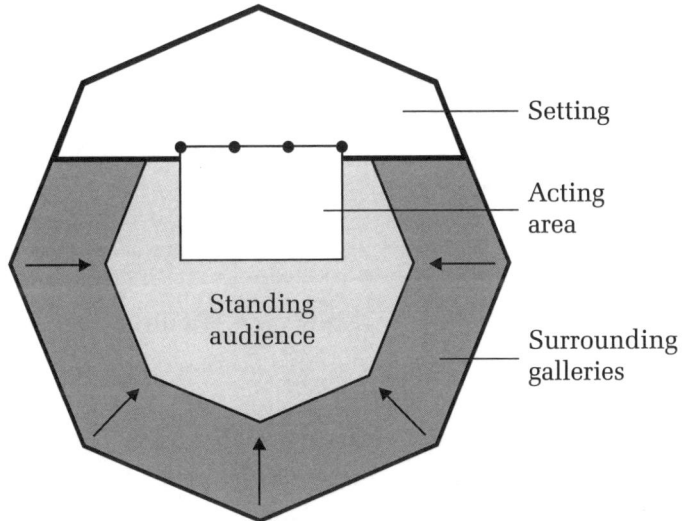

Web link

At least two important theatres from the end of this period survive in England: the Georgian Theatre Royal in Richmond, Yorkshire, built in 1788 (www.georgiantheatreroyal.co.uk) and the Regency Theatre Royal in Bury St Edmunds, opened in 1819 (www.theatreroyal.org).

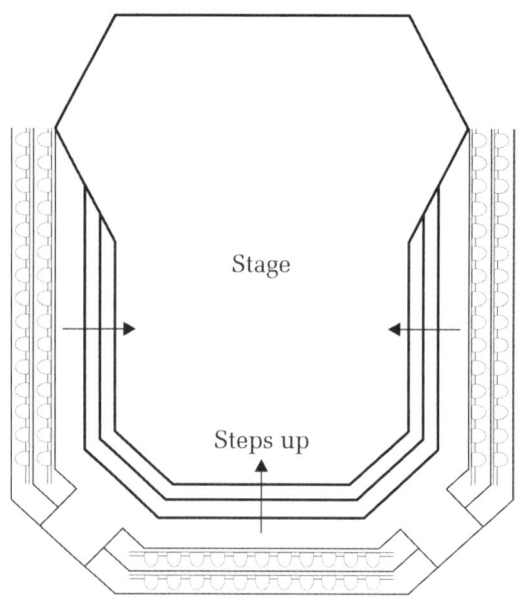

End-on theatre At this time, rich aristocrats often commissioned plays to be performed privately for themselves and their guests. These plays would be acted out in halls, such as those that survive in the colleges of Oxford and Cambridge. From this tradition, rather than the open-air tradition of the Globe, the theatre of the 17th and 18th centuries emerged: the **end-on theatre**, where the stage is at one of the short ends of a rectangle and the audience occupies the body of the rectangle and sometimes vantage points on the three facing walls.

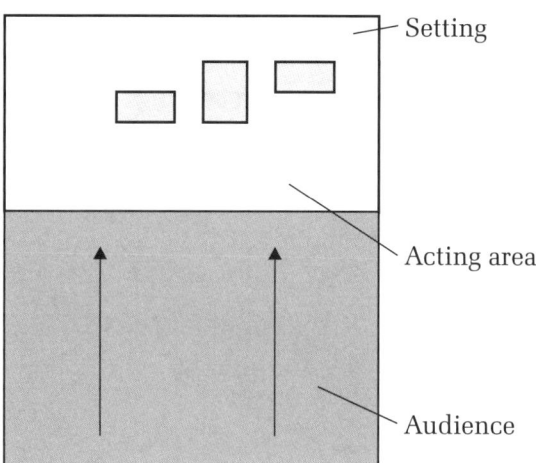

Proscenium arch As theatres grew in size, so the performing area grew more distinct from the audience, and the **proscenium arch** was built to frame the performers, so that the audience watched the show through the arch which was closed with a curtain for scene changes and at the ends of acts. The curtains which close across the proscenium arch are called **house tabs**. The **apron** of the stage is that section which protrudes in front of the proscenium arch. In plays from the 18th and 19th centuries, you can often see how dramatists structured their plays to take advantage of this system. Relatively long and detailed scenes taking place in clear settings such as living rooms or salons are alternated with exterior scenes which take place in the street and involve fewer characters or less action.

This is to allow a painted curtain to cover the stage area, while characters meet on the 'street' along the apron of the stage; when that scene is over, the curtain is drawn to reveal another carefully assembled interior.

> Sheridan's play *The Rivals* works well in this way, using such devices to allow time for scene changes.

Acts and scenes

In these terms, a **scene** is a practical division of the play into episodes, while an **act** is an artistic division revealing the structure of the play. It was traditional for people to take refreshment between the acts, and in some theatres of the 18th and 19th centuries (and later), where the wealthy and the fashionable met, this socialising often became more important than the play itself.

Modern staging

Modern theatre design tends to be flexible, so that performances can be given in ways that echo one or more of these more historical styles. As a result, other styles of staging have emerged:

➢ A **traverse stage** is one which runs between two auditorium areas, enabling action to sweep along it

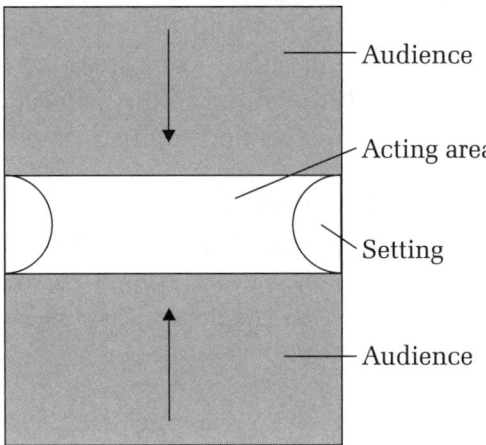

➢ A **promenade production** is one where the actors mingle with the audience, who have to walk around or 'promenade' in order to follow the action

➢ **Theatre in the round** is performed from a central stage with the auditorium like a doughnut around the outside, in a way reminiscent of an amphitheatre.

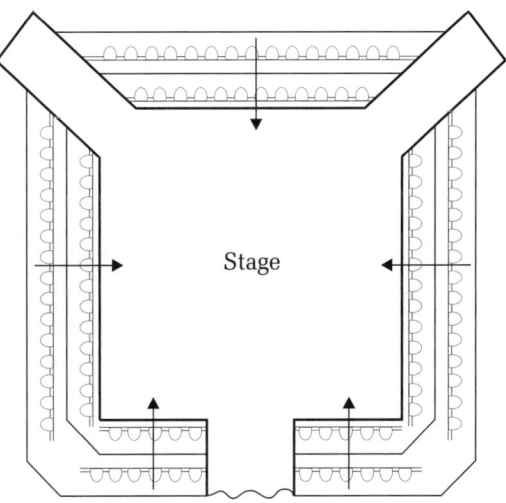

Modern directors are often free to adapt their performance space to suit the vision they have for the play that they are directing; each of these staging designs creates a different relationship between players and audience and entails different patterns of movement.

Upstage, downstage

> Directors use this terminology when working on the blocking of a play with actors, allowing them to give simple instructions to the actors as to where they should move.

A lot of the specialist vocabulary for describing the practical elements of a theatre derives from the proscenium arch theatres of the 18th century. In those days, the stage was often raked, so that the back, furthest from the audience, was raised a little. This enabled everyone to be able to see the action. As a result, the back of the stage in this sense is still called upstage and the front downstage. The terms stage left and stage right refer to the actor's left and right as they face the auditorium, which can be confusing!

Levels and backdrops

> A backdrop is a large cloth on which a realistic image is painted to suggest a location for a scene. These days backdrops are most commonly seen in pantomimes, where quick scene changes are required.

In this period, stage designers introduced features on the stage to create levels, which meant some actors could be higher than others, creating visual interest and some symbolic effect. It was also traditional to design a set with a significant backdrop upstage. In provincial theatres, where these existed, there was simply a collection of such backdrops, and the most appropriate were chosen and used; in London, gifted artists painted them to order. The melodramas of the 19th century – big, sentimental narrative plays – used incredibly effective and sophisticated backdrops.

Many modern productions dispense with backdrops. Often they are replaced by a cyclorama – a blank surface, cleverly or significantly lit, which runs behind the performing space. In some modern productions, the cyclorama is used as a screen for projected digital images.

> Wokingham Theatre has a stage area approximately 28' wide, 23' deep and 14' high. The apron protrudes 5' and extends stage right by another 4'. Stage left wing space is 9' by 23' and has the stage manager's desk behind the proscenium arch. Stage right is, again, 9' wide and 23' deep. There is a walkway behind the cyclorama wall to allow access to both sides of the stage. This wall is 34' wide and extends to full height. There is also a white cyclorama screen that covers the whole wall.

When touring companies are arranging their schedules, their managers need full details of the stages and theatres where they are to perform. Theatres provide detailed descriptions of their facilities. Here, on the left, is an extract from the details provided by one such theatre: you should be able to understand it all now!

Set

In Elizabethan times, there was little or no set in the theatre. As the years passed, however, designers began to pay more attention to designing the stage to suit the action taking place on it. They would use **stage plans** to ensure that their designs were practicable and allowed the plays to be performed. Often this included making models of the set to show what was required and how things would work.

Flats are painted scenery panels that are used to create different kinds of space on stage. Some of these are hung from the space at the top of the stage (the **flies**) and are called **flown scenery**; others may be fixed on wheels or **trucks** to enable movement. Some designers, especially during the 19th century when realism became fashionable, worked very hard to create **perspective** on stage. In some European productions, the designer even employed people of short stature to fill out the crowd upstage, so as to add to effects of perspective!

Stage plans

Flats

> Where flats are stationary, as in a traditional box set, they are held in place through a system of weights and braces.

Effects

Sometimes such scenery was extremely ambitious, a heritage which survives in the traditional West End productions of musicals in which big stage effects are often celebrated as ends in themselves. **Hydraulics** may be used to raise or lower whole areas of the stage in order to create such big effects; a **rain curtain** may be used to create the effect of rainfall by supplying a narrow shower of water which is collected in guttering and recycled (rarely without spillage and complications!). Sometimes, stages may **revolve**, allowing intricate scenery to change within minutes. Such productions often use a wealth of special effects.

There was, of course, little or no lighting in the theatre until relatively modern times – although it's worth remembering that it was a **pyrotechnic** (or firework) effect, designed to make the firing of a cannon more realistic, which led to the burning down of the Globe Theatre in 1613 – but now complex lighting is a key part in even the smallest production.

The **lighting plot** is the term given to the way the play is lit from beginning to end. The lighting designer must first arrange and focus the lanterns to create the **lighting rig** for this particular production. This will include the use of colour **gels** to create specific effects and of **gobos**, which are metal silhouettes placed in front of a lantern's lens so that shadows of a specific design are cast on the stage. In this way, a lighting designer can create the effects of moonlit windows, the dappled light of a forest and so on. Many students underestimate the importance of the lighting rig, and of colouring and focusing the light they are going to use. It is wise not to do so.

The lanterns can be shining from above the auditorium, perhaps from one of the higher levels of seating or from the side of the stage. Often they are held on a **gantry** which suspends them above

Lighting

Lanterns

the auditorium or above the stage itself. By varying the angle of the light beams, a lighting designer can create interesting and atmospheric visual effects. **Chiaroscuro** is an artistic term used to refer to an image that is dramatically lit in order to provide some brightly lit surfaces and some deep shadow.

There is a whole range of terms to describe the different lanterns available to a lighting designer and only the most common are glossed here:

- A flood provides a bland, unfocused light and, although popular, is the least useful stage lantern

- A fresnel lantern is much more versatile, using a special lens to create a soft pool of light

- A profile uses a different kind of lens to produce a sharp, narrow beam of light

- A parcan is a type of lantern which projects a light that is bright but unfocused and in an oval or elliptical shape

- A birdie is a small parcan used to light awkward corners of a set, or placed on the front of a stage to uplight faces and create interesting shadows on the cyclorama

- A strobe emits a regular series of high-power flashes (which can provoke epileptic fits in some individuals, hence warnings must be published in the theatre if a strobe light is to be used).

Lighting effects can be enhanced by the use of **gauze**, which is a coarsely woven cloth. When lit from the front, it is opaque; when lit from behind it becomes transparent. The effect is similar to net curtains in a house.

Sound

Just as a lighting plot contributes to the overall design of a play, so does a soundscape. This is where a collage of sound effects and music can create a kind of aural backdrop to some or all of the action.

It is important to remember that none of this design work should overshadow the role in a performance of the actor, whose speech and gestures communicate the play to the audience. In creating a character, an actor will use voice and body. Some playwrights, such as William Congreve, were famous in their day for creating distinctive 'voices' for their characters. A good actor will be sensitive to the **diction** or the choice of words given to a character. By finding an appropriate **accent** and **pitch**, a good actor can create a convincing speech pattern for a character.

> William Congreve (1670–1729) is considered one of the best comic dramatists of the Restoration period.

Drama theory and analysis

It will be helpful to know some of the key developments in the history of theatre and performance. Greek theatre is an obvious starting point. Greek theatre began at a festival held each spring in honour of Dionysus, the god of wine, youth and fertility. He was also a spirit of energy, action and violence, and a bringer of madness. Dionysus was the son of Zeus (a god) and Semele (a mortal). Semele was killed before Dionysus was born so Zeus took the baby from her body and planted it in his thigh. Later, Dionysus was born from Zeus's thigh – thus he was twice born. The hymn sung to Dionysus by his followers is the dithyramb, which means 'twice born'. Dionysus was a god of possession; he could reveal himself to his followers directly while they were in a state of ecstasis (trance). Worship was liberating for them and freed them from the constraints of society. This was directly opposite to the ordered Greek society, which was politically and socially sophisticated, aware of its own identity and proud of it. By worshipping Dionysus, the individual was allowed to question the very nature of society. This explains why the start of theatre in Greek society was so explosive: it jolted the audience into questioning the nature of their own existence, something that theatre has tended to do ever since. Greek drama asks questions of its audience, it seeks out the irrational in society and in the destiny of man. It demands that the audience experience that which cannot be rationalised. It does not provide the answers – the individual must do that for themselves – but it provides the experiences to allow the right questions to be asked. At the very centre of Greek drama is the conflict between man and god.

Origins of Greek theatre

The festival in Athens was a competition for performances of tragic plays with three performed each day (followed by a lighter satyr play to round off the day). The word tragedy comes from *tragoidia* meaning 'goat song', probably because a goat was originally given as a prize or sacrifice. Thespis, who is seen as the father of the theatre and after whom actors are named today (thespians), won this play competition in 534 BCE. It is thought that he was the first 'actor' to step forward from the chorus and take on one of the characters of the story. As the drama evolved Aeschylus (525–456 BCE) added a second actor, which allowed for greater conflict and plot, and then Sophocles (496–406 BCE) added a third, which enabled him to humanise the dialogue still further and to develop interplay between the actors. The chorus members were now used as witnesses and as lyrical commentators on the action, becoming the link between the audience and the play, asking the questions the audience should be asking of themselves. The dramatic conflict becomes one that seemingly has right on both sides and, when no compromise is given, must end in disaster for both sides.

Dramatic festivals

The ancient Greek philosopher Aristotle (384–322 BCE) explored the genre of tragedy in his work of literary criticism, the Poetics. His discussion was hugely influential on the tragedies of the Elizabethan and Jacobean ages. Aristotle thought that a tragedy should involve a protagonist of high estate who falls from

Aristotle and tragedy

> 'Jacobean' refers to the age of James I of England, VI of Scotland (reigned in England 1603–1625).

prosperity to misery through a series of discoveries, as the result of a tragic flaw which is usually based on moral or human weakness. According to Aristotle, the action of the play should include:

- **Revolution**: the unanticipated reversal of what is expected to occur

- **Discovery**: a turning point in the play when the protagonist and the audience learn something that had previously been hidden

- **Disasters**: here all the destructive actions and deaths occur.

Aristotle thought that to be tragedy, a play should invoke pity and fear in the audience. He suggested that the audience were allowed to find a kind of release from their own pent-up emotions in seeing similar emotions exaggerated to breaking-point in performance. He called this release **catharsis**.

Development of drama

As theatre developed in Europe – from classical times, through the Medieval and Renaissance periods, the Age of Enlightenment and the 19th century, to the developments of the 20th century – so the style of play and the style of performance also developed.

> Shakespeare mocks this kind of classification of plays in *Hamlet*, Act 2, scene 2.

Following the prominence of religious plays in medieval times, the renaissance in western Europe rediscovered the ancient play-texts, and playwrights once again became explicitly interested in writing comedy and tragedy. They also explored mixing the styles, producing plays with tragic openings and happy endings; people call such plays **tragi-comedies**.

Verbal imagery

The Elizabethan period (1558–1603) or late Renaissance – the era in which Shakespeare came to prominence in England (and Lope de Vega and Cervantes in Spain) – provided very little scenery or effects in its theatres. Instead, the job was done by verbal imagery. Sometimes – in a modern production with a full set and design plan, or in a film, for example – Shakespeare's language can seem slow and redundant, for all its beauty. But his poetic imagery was feeding the imagination of his audience; he needed to remind them over and over again that Romeo and Juliet were meeting at night, because his play was being performed under an afternoon sky. In a modern theatre, where the lights are dimmed and dark shadows fill the stage, this repetition can seem to slow the play down, but in its original context, it was vital.

Rhythm

Many of these plays were written in verse. This has many merits, but an important one – often neglected or undervalued – concerns the ease with which a rhythmic line can be **projected** by the actor's voice. Getting the words of Hamlet across audibly in a Shakespearean theatre was made much easier by giving each line a rhythmic balance and pulse. In English, the **iambic pentameter** (five unstressed syllables alternating with five stressed ones) turned out to be perfect for this.

The **Jacobean** period in England, and the baroque period on the continent, witnessed the further polarisation of the two genres of tragedy and comedy. In England, Jacobean tragedy is notorious for its violence and cruelty; but some comedies embraced the values of the court **masque**, which was almost performance for performance's sake. Similar extravagances are found in European plays of this period, including those from the 'Golden Age' in Spain by playwrights such as Calderón de la Barca and Tirso de Molina.

> The baroque period was the 17th and early 18th century. Its literature, art and music often explored rich, ornate effects and celebrated extremes.

Restoration comedies

The European comedy of the late 17th and 18th century was essentially sexual in theme, dealing with the relationships between men and women among the relaxed and decadent mores of the moneyed classes. The English stage now had actresses – up until this point, women's parts had been played by boys – and playwrights took every advantage of this change. These plays, often called **Restoration comedies** in England (where Charles II had been restored to the throne in 1660) were almost always **comedies of manners**, at once celebrating and mocking the values of the audience that had come to watch. Such a style remained popular throughout the Georgian period. These plays were often set in interiors and performed in intimate theatres, as we have seen. Therefore, they lent themselves to the use of prose in their speeches. However, this prose was not a true reflection of the way people naturally spoke at this time: it was still carefully poised and artfully balanced, to emphasise the wit of the language and the ideas. It is not, in the end, very much more realistic than verse.

Further reading

Examples include William Wycherley's *The Country Wife* and *The Plain Dealer*, Farquhar's *The Recruiting Officer*, as well as Congreve's *Love for Love* and *The Way of the World*.

> 'Georgian' refers to the period of the reigns of the four Georges from 1714 to 1830.

Realism

During the 19th century, there developed a much greater emphasis on **realism** – making things look and sound as they do in real life. Many theatre companies spent enormous amounts of time and money creating the realistic appearance of the play's setting. Gerhart Hauptmann's play *The Weavers* is just one of a number of plays from this period that require very complex and detailed settings. Other playwrights, though, demanded a simpler kind of realism. The plays of Henrik Ibsen (1828–1906), for example, demand accurate Scandinavian interiors.

> Hauptmann (1862–1946) was a prominent German dramatist who won the Nobel prize for literature in 1912. *The Weavers* (1893) is one of his best known works.

Stock characters

The result of this movement towards realism was the need for a fundamentally different kind of acting. The comedies of manners of the 18th and 19th centuries relied on **stock characters** and **stock situations**. Actors used **stock gestures** – clasping their hands to their breast, for example, at moments of high passion – and played in clothes they liked, rather than in costumes that suited their characters.

Commedia dell'arte

In some ways, this style of acting was part of a tradition that dated back to the **commedia dell'arte** of the late Italian renaissance, which came to have an important influence on theatre throughout Europe. As performers of commedia used stock masks to represent their characters, this led to a very physical style of exaggerated comic acting. Commedia plays were largely improvised in public places, and their plots involved the interaction of a group of stock characters, including the beautiful young woman Columbina and the greedy merchant Pantalone. Wit, topicality and physical humour were important elements of the commedia.

Stanislavski

This kind of approach did not suit a realistic writer like Ibsen or Chekhov and ran counter to their aims. A significant change in acting style was now essential. In the end, the work of the Russian director Constantin Stanislavski represented this revolution in acting. He saw that realism worked through **metonymy**, which is the suggestion of a whole through the revelation just of parts. He devised a series of approaches to the text that allowed the actors to explore the devices of metonymy used in the play, so that they could create psychologically realistic characters.

Naturalism

Growing out of realism, **naturalism** was a philosophical approach to life that derived from Charles Darwin's work in biology. Naturalist writers, such as Émile Zola in France, Henrik Ibsen in Norway and Thomas Hardy in England, followed Darwin's view that people (or species) were created by a combination of heredity and environment. Their writings placed great emphasis on parentage and on location in exploring character and motive.

Naturalist plays usually present a tense situation, whereby one small intervention from outside will strain things to breaking point. The play describes the situation, the intervention, the tension, the breaking point and the aftermath. They use realism to emphasise their naturalism, presenting their intimate scenes in realistic settings, so that it is as if the 'fourth wall' of the room has been peeled away allowing the audience to peer in.

Metaphor

Inevitably, dramatists began to enjoy the effects of exploring the kind of deep, repressed emotion which the naturalists were tapping into. The **Expressionist** writers of the early 20th century articulated often extreme emotion and dramatised it through symbol and metaphor. Sometimes, this metaphor went well beyond reality and became **surreal**, like the imagery of dreams and the art of the Surrealists, or **absurd**. Actors in such plays often had to be athletic and able to discover profound emotions on stage, as Antonin Artaud recognised. This preference for metaphor over metonymy was a characteristic of the **modernist** movement. Metonymy shows what something looks like: metaphor reveals what it is, modernists might say.

Symbolism

Other playwrights rejected this extremism and wrote **symbolist** plays, whose meanings were less precise, hinted at with imagery that was often visual or musical, rather than explicit. The verse plays of W. B. Yeats are typical of symbolist drama.

> **Further study**
>
> Find out what the expression 'agit prop' means and think how it might be used in a theatrical context.

By the second half of the 20th century, theatre had become rich and varied: former styles of writing and performing, including a continued interest in putting on **period plays** (old plays in the style associated with them), were existing side by side with more experimental work. **Political theatre** set out to alert the audience to social and economic issues, using populist techniques such as song, as well as **polemic** – politically explicit persuasive language. **Physical theatre** moved away from the power of the written script to embrace movement and dance elements. **Community theatre** valued the cooperation of a community in a production more than professionalism and perfection in performance.

Understanding the text

Identifying forms and characters

When writing about a play, we need to use some specialist vocabulary in order to make our comments precise and specific. Obviously, we are already able to use terms such as **character** and **role**, but there are other aspects of characterisation that you will need to be able to identify and label. When identifying the main character in the play – if there is one – you can refer to them as the **hero**, even if they don't do anything very heroic. Another term that you might prefer is **protagonist**, which draws attention to the fact that your character instigates the action. Then you might call the key character whose life is affected as a result of the action of the protagonist, the **antagonist**. When the hero is actually nothing like a hero, but displays characteristics which are in fact pretty negative or despicable, you can refer to them as the **anti-hero**.

You may find that when characters first appear, the playwright suggests certain **stereotypical** features about them, so that we can recognise quickly what kind of people they are. Usually, as the play develops, these stereotypical features are modified and made more interesting.

When looking at a script, you may need to identify a number of different forms or structures. A **monologue**, for example, is a fairly long, significant speech delivered by one character. Sometimes a monologue is delivered to other characters on stage. If it is delivered to the audience alone, it has a specific name, a **soliloquy**. A **duologue** is a name for a section of text where two characters speak to one another; **dialogue** is the term for any section of conversation involving two or more characters. An **aside** is a rather artificial device whereby an actor comments directly to the audience, apparently unheard by the other actors, however close by they may be standing.

We can also analyse features of the text. The **plot**, of course, is the sequence of events that structure the play; the **subplot** is a second, subordinate section of the story that almost stands on its own, and which complements the main plot – either by repeating some of its themes though handling them differently (as in *King Lear*) or by developing contrasting ones (as in *Twelfth Night*). When a subplot provides a humorous element that contrasts with the serious main plot, we may call this an example of **comic relief**.

You might also want to structure your thoughts about the whole play or each individual scene by locating within it certain elements of basic narrative. For example, first there is a **situation**, explained by an initial **exposition**. This is in due course interrupted by a **complication**. (Sometimes this leads to a whole series of advances and **reversals**.) This then leads to a **crisis** and then to a climax. After the climax there is a **resolution** or a **denouement**, which ends the play or scene.

Characters

> When talking about all the roles in a play, you can use the Latin term 'dramatis personae', which translates as 'the people of the play'.

Forms

Features

> Exposition is where characters reveal their back-story, the important background information about themselves or the situation they are in.

> **Further study**
>
> Denouement is a French term which translates as 'untying'. It is part of the analysis of the 'well-made play', set out by the French playwright Eugène Scribe. See what you can find out about his five-act structure, and why he coined the term. Can it, or should it, be applied to all plays?

Sometimes, the denouement may feel rather contrived. In many Greek plays, when the situation within the play had become very complicated, an actor representing a god appeared, suspended from some sort of crane, to resolve everything. A phrase emerged from this: **deus ex machina**. This Latin phrase means 'a god from a machine', but now it is used to mean any sudden, rather unconvincing conclusion. For example, a letter might arrive that somehow sorts out a complicated situation quickly, but unconvincingly.

Style and genre

One key challenge facing a performer, a director or a designer when confronted by a new or unfamiliar text is to identify both **genre** and **style**. This will help them understand how its meanings are to be conveyed. It's thus probably helpful to be clear about the difference between genre and style. Genre describes the kind of play we are dealing with: words that describe genre include tragedy, comedy, **satire** and **melodrama**. Some genre terms are more specific than others (melodrama, for example, relates to a very specific type of play), some, like tragedy, have provoked debate and some controversy and can refer to a large variety of plays.

Options Style refers to the options chosen by a director when presenting the play on stage, which includes both the manner of performance and the production elements such as setting and costume design. In other words a comedy (genre) might be presented on stage in the style of a pantomime or in the style of physical theatre. Style can also relate more directly to the historical period in which a play was first produced, so that when we say that *A Midsummer Night's Dream* is performed in a Shakespearean style, we will be expecting a classically Elizabethan production. However, a director might choose to present the play out of its historical style, to reveal other levels of meaning. When we go to see a production of a familiar play, what interests us is often no longer the story but the new interpretation, which invites us to revisit the text and see something new in it.

Spotting the features of style in a play, therefore, requires experience and wider reading. The type of language, for example, will help us identify the style of performance. Can a verse play be played realistically? Can a play full of witty jokes be expected to move its audience to tears? How has the writer hinted at voice and tone? As a director should you always follow the style of the writing when deciding how to present your production, or can it be advantageous to go against the written style to make a particular point to your audience?

Subtext

People don't always say what they mean. In our ordinary lives, we can feel insulted by silence. Playwrights (and actors) love this. When we read a new scene, we can ask ourselves, do these people mean exactly what they say, or are they hinting at something else? This hidden message – the **subtext** – provides great interest for us all. A lot of the enjoyment an audience gets in the theatre concerns the use of subtext. When characters don't say what they mean, or give away what they're feeling by saying something improbable, the audience loves to solve the problem and to work out exactly what it is that makes these characters tick.

Dramatic intention

By looking at a text in this way we can begin to ask ourselves what the writer's **dramatic intention** is. Do not think of a play as a novel written for the stage. A playwright uses all of the stage's potential to create their meanings. Silent characters, small props, the painted view out of a small window: all these contribute to dramatic effect, so be sensitive to them.

Themes

After you have read a text, you will be able to understand something about its **themes**, the abstract or intellectual ideas behind the drama. In a realistic drama we tend to see the action as being part of a bigger social issue; in a more poetic drama, it is up to us to interpret the action and find the deeper meaning. Playwrights often use **symbolism** to help create meaning and develop themes: it is one of their most powerful tools, allowing them to use seemingly ordinary events and actions to highlight a more significant issue. For example, if you see someone eating an apple in the auditorium you might rightly just assume they are having a snack: if you see someone eating an apple on stage, it could be reference to Adam and Eve, and thus to all sorts of themes such as the nature of sin, creation and so on.

Analogy and allegory

Sometimes, scenes in a play offer a kind of simplified version of a complex issue. By creating such an **analogy**, the playwright is able to create more meaning. Sometimes, the analogy is so overarching that the whole play works on a completely different level: then it becomes an **allegory**. The characters in an allegory sometimes have no individual personality at all, but simply embody the issues or moral qualities involved.

David Edgar's play *Pentecost* begins with a Balkan art expert removing bricks from the back wall of an old church so that she can show a visiting English art professor a remarkable medieval painting. This can be interpreted as a symbol for the cultural heritage running behind the problems in the Balkans; the relationship between the woman and the man seems to have something of an allegory about it, replicating perhaps the relationship between the Balkans and the West. In this way, one of Edgar's dramatic intentions – that of alerting his audience to the political issues of the Balkans – is already clear after the first few minutes.

Audience reaction

When we read a text like Edgar's, therefore, we are already beginning to form an interpretation of it, based on our understanding of the intentions we read behind the writing. We balance a whole range of different signals: language, stage action, characters, gesture and so on, to create our own reading of the play.

However, the final summing up of an interpretation concerns the audience: how do we want them to respond? Do we want them just want to be entertained? Do we want them to be horrified, to experience some sort of catharsis? Do we want them to laugh at one another, or themselves? Do we want them to think about something? This final interpretation needs to be mapped on to the text. You must guard against jumping to quick conclusions about a character or about the function of a speech and then forcing other elements of a text into line with these initial misconceptions. Keep testing your ideas against the text so that your conclusions are water-tight.

Unit 3a: Pre-20th Century Texts

Analysing a set text

As you study a set text, you will need to gain a thorough understanding of its content, language, structure, characterisation, setting and so on. However, you will also need to develop some ideas about how to turn this understanding into a concrete performance. In this sense, the text merely represents one stage in the process of staging a play.

You will need to develop a series of techniques to achieve this conversion from conceptual text to concrete performance, and use them to offer analyses of the play text and to give a rationale for your dramatic decisions. Reading the text is essential, of course, but it is not enough in itself; you will need to rehearse the text, too.

Your answers in the exam will have to map the journey from text to stage and you will need to provide a rationale for all your suggestions. It is surprising how often one meets directorial suggestions (both on examination papers and in real life) which lack any coherent sense of a rationale. Examination essays will often include phrases such as 'at this stage in the play, Dorothy will be wearing a long gown and will utter her lines nervously'. This is not the right approach at all. Having studied the text, you should be able to imagine a spectrum of different approaches, each of which will have its own, subtly different rationale.

A better answer would say: 'a director *may* want to emphasise the sense of anxiety Dorothy feels at this time in order to stress the importance of Anthony's arrival.' This sentence is better for a number of reasons:

> Other modal verbs which are useful for this effect include 'might', 'could' and 'would'.

- Firstly, the use of the modal verb 'may' places you at a distance from the suggestion, thereby acknowledging the existence of other interpretations

- Secondly, you have indicated that two directors will not necessarily reach the same solutions for the problems the play text poses

- Finally, your suggestion for performance has clearly been shaped by your understanding of the conceptual structure of the play.

> Where relevant, you might like to answer the question from two viewpoints: 'one director, seeking a more abstract interpretation of the play, may do this, another, taking a more realistic approach, may do that' and so on.

Approaching the text

For each text we study we need an approach which will allow us to uncover its different levels of meaning and structure, explore how these can be conveyed on stage in a concrete performance, relating them to each other to make an intellectually and artistically satisfying production and, finally, enable us to write an A-grade essay in the examination!

Ideas for production can be broken down into any number of elements. However, the following four are the most useful in treating a text at the level required for A2 study:

- Character
- Set
- Costumes and props
- Ideas in action.

To create an effective production of a play, these four elements must lean sensitively and intelligently on the material contained in the text itself. Some of this material may be explicit – the actor's lines or descriptions of set and props, for example – while some of it may be implicit.

Different directors will place different emphases on the layers of ideas which a rich play will contain. You need to be sensitive to these various layers and aware that two directors will present two different but equally valid readings of a text; ultimately, you also need to have some clear ideas of your own about how *you* would present the text as a play in performance.

When you know your play well, you will be able to clarify for yourself what its central ideas are and how to puts these into action. Decide which are the two or three key ideas your 'virtual' production will emphasise, and why. Make sure, however, that you do not fall into the trap of thinking that your own production represents the only set of solutions for the problems which the play poses; an exam question may surprise you by requiring you to think along unexpected lines.

Practical exercise

Having read carefully through the play you are studying, record your thoughts about precisely what happens in it. While you may want to work individually on this task, it might be more efficient to divide the work among your group and to organise a sharing of ideas in a series of presentations to one another.

It's a good idea to identify key moments in the play. The exam questions will, after all, often invite you to choose key moments on which to build your answer.

The Revenger's Tragedy

Introduction to the play

The Revenger's Tragedy is a Jacobean tragedy. While its authorship is uncertain (it has been attributed to both Cyril Tourneur and Thomas Middleton), it almost certainly dates from the first decade of the 17th century. It shares the revenge motifs of Shakespeare's *Hamlet* and the violence-on-stage of *King Lear*.

The play is written in verse and incorporates aphorisms and proverbs as verbal motifs throughout. The characters have names which echo, in an Italianate Latin, their roles in the play: for example, the 'revenger' is called Vindice (although we should note that nearly every character becomes involved in some form of vendetta), and his honest sister is called Castiza ('chastity').

Further viewing

There has even been a recent film version of the play: *Revenger's Tragedy* directed by Alex Cox and starring Derek Jacobi and Christopher Eccleston (Tartan Video 2003).

In 1966, the Royal Shakespeare Theatre revived the play under the direction of Trevor Nunn. Some critics refer to this as the first time the play was performed for 450 years, while others refer to a production in Pitlochry in 1965, directed by Brian Shelton. Certainly the Trevor Nunn production re-established the play in the repertoire and it is still widely performed today.

Senecan tradition

The Revenger's Tragedy sits firmly within a Senecan tradition. Little is known about Seneca's life. Some writers assert that he was born in Córdoba in Andalusia, southern Spain. He seems to have arrived in Rome as a very young boy, and as an adult he worked as a tutor and a counsellor to the emperor Caligula and later to Nero. Inevitably, given the nature of Roman politics at the time, he became embroiled in dynastic squabbles and conspiracy. Justly or not, he was accused of plotting, and he and his wife were forced to commit suicide.

> In his works, Seneca adopted the views of the stoic philosophers: man is born to suffer, and suffering must be borne.

Seneca's plays became the model for Elizabethan and consequently Jacobean theatre in England. Dramatists followed his five-act structure and his favour for revenge as a motivation for action. This led to the inclusion of violent action – often depicted on stage – and long soliloquies in which characters explore their thoughts, emotions and desires. He often used supernatural elements, which also appear in Shakespearean drama: the witches, for instance, in *Macbeth* and the ghost in *Hamlet*. Through its verse, its five-act structure, its themes of violence and dynastic struggle, its lurid depiction of violence on stage, and the fact that it ends with the deaths of nearly all of the major characters, *The Revenger's Tragedy* belongs firmly in an 'English Senecan' tradition.

> One problem for 17th-century dramatists was that Seneca was writing for a pagan world, whereas England was a long-established Christian country. In many of the plays which bear his influence, there is a juxtaposition of Senecan and Christian values (for example, Hamlet resists killing his uncle at prayer to prevent his soul flying straight to heaven).

Modern productions

Caroline May, a playwright and critic, in reviewing a production at the Manchester Royal Exchange, compares the play to a 'favourite action movie':

> *The Revenger's Tragedy* is a classic example of the genre, containing as it does the key ingredients that any dedicated fan would expect to see on the poster: murder, rape, incest, adultery, pimping, poisoning and necrophilia – frankly, what's not to like? ... Scholars may dispute the authorship – it could be by Cyril Tourneur, it might be by Thomas Middleton – but my own theory is that it's an early lost work by Quentin Tarantino.

Web link

Read this review in its entirety by visiting www.uktheatre.tv and searching for 'the revenger's tragedy'.

The play's subject matter and its breaking of social, moral and dramatic taboos from start to finish certainly makes modern critics lean towards this sort of reading. Its setting in Italy is significant. Italy in the 17th century was a wealthy, foreign land notorious for feuds, violence and its sex industry. By setting plays in this locale, playwrights bought into a sensationalised fictional space, much in the same way that screenwriters today may set their drug-land quarrels in a fictionalised Los Angeles.

Modern directors often feel the need to justify a play whose violence and cruelty have gained it a certain notoriety. Trevor Nunn wanted his audience to see something of the 1960s in his groundbreaking

1966 production, noting that the play is 'extraordinarily about aspects of our world ... where the relationship between sex, violence and money was becoming increasingly popular'. In his introduction to the play, R. A. Foakes amplifies this, adding that the play 'is every bit as relevant now [1996] and as disturbing'.

The director's role is to create the nightmarish world in which *The Revenger's Tragedy* takes place. The play gives few concrete clues about set: even when we move from the Duke's court to Vindice's home, there is little significant change in the milieu. The ease with which characters disguise themselves – the Duke mistakes a skull in a gown for a courtesan – suggests a twilit world of shadows and half-light, or a kind of 'Caravaggio on stage'. Directors are therefore given great scope when coming to design their production of the play.

> **Further reading**
>
> *The Revenger's Tragedy* edited by R. A. Foakes (Manchester University Press 1996).
>
> See *Quentin Tarantino* by Ed Gallafent (Longman 2006). Are there any ideas suggested by this book which could be used in a stage production of a Jacobean revenge tragedy?

In 2003, Samantha Ellis of *The Guardian* wrote an 'art history' piece in which she re-evaluated the impact of Nunn's 1966 production. She focused significantly on how contemporary critics responded to the design element:

> *The Daily Mail*'s Peter Lewis ... liked Nunn's 'coldly fascinating' production ... but was most enthusiastic about Christopher Morley's costumes: 'He has dressed this odious crew with fantasy and elegance in silver and black cloaks and steel-wool wigs so that they float through the darkness like evil moths.' Other critics also liked the production's glossy look; *the Stage* called it 'a magnificent swirl of glinting silver, grey and black'.

One of the chief roles of a director of this play is to establish, on the one hand, the play's relevance – it can be viewed as a kind of dramatisation of a lurid Sunday paper – and, on the other, its otherworldly location.

Staging the play: key moments

By examining three key moments in more detail, we can chart the dramatic patterns of the play and identify sections which would make excellent starting points for rehearsal and exploration of the text.

The opening

The image created in the opening scene is a strong one. It is dark; Vindice watches as a torch-lit procession of nobles crosses the stage, led by the Duke against whom he seeks revenge. From the very start we see Vindice as a man of the shadows, his business that of the night-time and the dark. Moreover, he is an outsider looking on; his opening speech simply reinforces this.

> In one or two recent productions, directors have interpolated business before the opening monologue. Although they have done so with the intention of creating an image world for the play, this has not generally gone down well with critics who found the added material diluted the impact of the opening.

In the very first few pages, the play covers a whole range of taboo behaviour: violence, revenge, rape and corruption. It begins by providing language which suggests a parody of ritual. Instead of a formal greeting to a respected lord and leader, we get a sophisticated curse:

> Duke, royal lecher; go, grey-haired adultery;
>
> And thou his son, as impious steeped as he;
>
> And thou his bastard, true-begot in evil;
>
> And thou his Duchess, that will do with the devil;
>
> Four excellent characters!

An actor preparing this role needs to be sensitive, of course, to the nuances in this speech. The use of the familiar second person – all those 'thous' – is itself an insult. But there are other questions for an actor and director. What should the tone of voice be like here? Loud and defiant or whispered like old radio commentaries of royal occasions?

The verse has a strong rhythm and end rhymes which add to the ritual flavour of the curse. An actor needs to play with this rhythm. There is a tendency in some modern productions of verse dramas to play down the verse and turn each speech into something with the prosaic feel of ordinary conversation. While that is not appropriate here, moving in that direction might help us to gauge exactly where to pitch the rhythms of the verse.

> Scholars and religious figures were often depicted with skulls on their desks, intended to remind them of their mortality and to guard against hubris; *memento mori* means 'a reminder of death'.

By line 14, it is clear that Vindice, in an image familiar from *Hamlet* and from late 16th-century painting, is talking to a skull, a *memento mori* from his study. And, to complete the macabre opening, we learn that it is the skull of his erstwhile lover, Gloriana, whom the Duke had poisoned because she would not consent to sleep with him.

Vindice reaches a conclusion in his train of thought at line 38 where he says, 'Age, as in gold, in lust is covetous'. Throughout the text the playwright uses this device of an **aphorism**, presented as an unequivocal assertion, to conclude a speech. It has a thematic effect in that it suggests that proverbial and rather cynical wisdom has replaced Christian morality or, indeed, any other system of values in the play's world. It has a dramatic effect, too, which director and actor need to explore. The whole of this opening speech is a soliloquy, of course, but it is not really directed at the audience, until this point. First, Vindice curses the members of the ducal procession, apparently oblivious to the presence of an audience. He then addresses the skull. Only at line 38 is there a suggestion that the audience is being addressed; they are likely to concur with his statement and are therefore drawn, unwittingly into his view of the world as he schemes his revenge.

Think about...

Where else are aphorisms used in *The Revenger's Tragedy*? How and why are they used?

Act 3 scene 5

The Duke's murder is a gruesome scene. He is poisoned and as he dies, he is tortured by having his tongue pinned by a dagger and by being forced to watch the incestuous sexual union between his wife and his illegitimate son. A director will need to think about how to manage these two grimly offensive images.

>
> **Further reading**
>
> There is a definite connection between *The Revenger's Tragedy* and *Hamlet*. It might prove valuable to see what use Shakespeare makes of similar generic features. (Trevor Nunn's revival of *The Revenger's Tragedy*, for financial reasons, had to use sets previously employed by a production of *Hamlet*, after all.)

>
> **Think about...**
>
> The episode with Spurio and the Duchess begins with just such a kiss. Would it be possible to physically echo the pose adopted by the Duke?

>
> **Practical exercise**
>
> Try performing the murder scene in Act 3 scene 5 with Nicholas Brooke's comment in mind.

Act 5 scene 3

Once again, we are in near darkness. The Duke is not going to be fooled – surely – by the manikin in broad daylight, nor are the lovers going to meet each other openly. Some directors add considerable staging effects to this scene, particularly as Vindice prepares his ruse and his weapons. They have good reason. Vindice has been waiting for nine years for his revenge and it is unlikely that he is going to rush things now. The deliberation with which the murder is accomplished is part of its horror, of course, but it is also part of a grotesque humour which emerges from time to time in the play.

The humour in *The Revenger's Tragedy* is perhaps more apparent in performance than on the page, but if you look you will find it in the text. For instance, Vindice presents the doll to the Duke with a crude pun which we may be familiar with from *Hamlet*: 'Faith my lord, a country lady' but then goes on to embrace his brother (and by extension, the audience) with another pun: 'She has somewhat a grave look with her, but –'. The comment may tail off here because the Duke interrupts, however it may also be to give its rather sick humour a chance to register. Such humour (if 'humour' is quite the right word) continues with the brother's feigned surprise that the Duke has any teeth left and with their mockery of his 'Dutch kissing'.

R. A. Foakes writes about the 'black comedy' of *The Revenger's Tragedy* in his introduction to the play. He recognises an almost Brechtian 'alienation effect' in its use of humour: 'The mode of *The Revenger's Tragedy* prevents the audience from a full sympathetic identification with the characters ... demanding an intellectual rather than an emotional engagement with its conscious theatrical artifice'. He goes on to quote Nicholas Brooke: 'The opposed possibilities of laughter and horror are both fully realised.' As an example of this he refers to the scene in which Lussurioso pulls back a curtain to reveal what he believes will be Spurio and the Duchess in a sexual embrace, only to find his parents in bed.

The playwright of *The Revenger's Tragedy* eventually seems to prioritise ritualised slaying over any sensible plotting. Preparations for the denouement are fleeting but effective enough in practice, and the audience is not really given time to consider their validity or otherwise. The brothers, Ambitioso and Supervacuo, with Spurio and a fourth accomplice, plan to take the part of the 'masquers' and kill Lussurioso in order to inherit – their plan to have him executed in prison having backfired. Hippolito and Vindice, with other accomplices, plan to kill Lussurioso for his part in trying to seduce their sister and for his closeness to the Duke. They manage to make costumes identical to those which will be worn by the 'masquers' and their dance takes place first.

In a similar fashion to the way in which dark humour undercuts the murder of the Duke, here we are offered a parody of the masques with which comedies of the period often ended (for instance, Shakespeare's *The Tempest*, to give just one example). The stage direction at line 40 says it all: 'The revengers dance; at the end, steal out their swords, and these four kill the four at the table in their chairs. It thunders.' It seems as if Caroline May has a point: this really is Quentin Tarantino territory.

There is some significant symbolism here, too. At the end of the play, Vindice and his brother have become literally indistinguishable from their victims, and the dynasty – in the form of Antonio – rapidly organises its revenge on them. If the play has a moral, it is that a desire for revenge turns us all into monsters: this is perhaps a different message, however, from that delivered by the play's content.

Questions and topics to think about

- What does the play have to say about gender roles?

- How would a director and designer use lighting to enhance the impact of the play?

- What style of stage – Jacobean, proscenium arch and so on – might a director choose for this play, and why?

- Which speech would you, as a director, choose as an audition piece for each of the main characters and why? How, as an actor, might you prepare for such an audition?

- Draw up a list of technical terms which would be needed for an in-depth discussion of the play.

- As a director, what ideas would you have for a creative overview of the play? What aspects of the text would you draw upon?

Questions you might expect in the exam

- As a director, how would you want the audience to respond to the death of the Duke?

- As an actor, how would you perform the part of the Duke in order to achieve this kind of response? Refer to the death scene and to one other.

- As a designer, discuss your rationale for creating an appropriate style and atmosphere for the play. (Think about at least two aspects of design: setting, including style of stage; costume; lighting.)

- How could this rationale be turned into practical staging applications?

- In which scene of the play might a director or an actor find the greatest problems in realising the play? Explain what these problems are and suggest practical solutions.

Tartuffe

Introduction to the play

Tartuffe by Molière is a short play with a long history. The reasons for it being banned when it was first performed in 1664 and again, even more stringently, in 1667 are complex; they involve not only the morality of 17th-century France but also the personal and political enemies Molière had made during his career as an actor and playwright. The chief objection to the play, however, was its depiction of moral and religious hypocrisy in a way which borders on satire. Political and religious leaders may have recognised in the character of Tartuffe something of the hypocrisy with which they were familiar and which they tolerated.

For English students of the play, it may be helpful to think of Molière attacking the values of Puritan hypocrisy and espousing the more libertarian – if not libertine – values of the Reformation.

The play dramatises a contemporary debate between over-devout, Pharisaic Christians and the libertines, those who believed in free thought and a fresh re-evaluation of orthodox morality. In *Tartuffe*, it is Cléante who best articulates the views of this new, radical outlook on life.

The playwright

Molière holds a prestigious place in the history of French drama. He was probably born early in 1622. His given name was Jean-Baptiste Poquelin; he called himself Molière around the time he joined L'Illustre Théâtre in Paris. In 1658, the company worked with Italian commedia dell'arte players, working in a tradition which Molière was to make French and his own. In 1661, the company took up residence in the theatre of the Palais-Royal near the Louvre Palace in central Paris. Molière's closeness to the king – Louis XIV, 'the Sun King' – is evidenced by the fact that he received a handsome royal pension and that the King became the godfather to Molière's son Louis. This patronage seems to be celebrated in the denouement of *Tartuffe*. This did not stop the King from banning *Tartuffe*, of course!

Further reading

The Cambridge Companion to Molière edited by David Bradby and Andrew Calder (Cambridge University Press 2006) provides a detailed study of the man, his theatre and his career.

After the King's death, the Comédie-Française was established in 1628, by the amalgamation of his company with the other main Parisian company. Comédie-Française's tradition of presenting plays by Molière and Racine began at this time and continues to the present day.

Web link

www.comedie-francaise.fr

Language

Molière wrote *Tartuffe* in rhyming Alexandrines, 12-syllable lines. The rhyming alternates between feminine rhymes (unstressed final vowel) and masculine rhymes (stressed final vowel). There seems little consensus in England about how best to translate this verse form into English.

Web link

You can assess the text at: http://abu.cnam.fr/cgi-bin/go?tartuf2,21,40

Let's have a look at the opening lines of the play in the original French.

Madame Pernelle:	Allons, Flipote, allons, que d'eux je me délivre.
Elmire:	Vous marchez d'un tel pas qu'on a peine à vous suivre.
Madame Pernelle:	Laissez, ma bru, laissez, ne venez pas plus loin:
	Ce sont toutes façons dont je n'ai pas besoin.
Elmire:	De ce que l'on vous doit envers vous on s'acquitte,
	Mais ma mère, d'où vient que vous sortez si vite?

Practical exercise

Read through these lines aloud. The long line, which is significantly longer than the Shakespearean iambic pentameter, takes away some of the 'drum kit' effect from the rhyme. Try to feel the pulse of the rhythm, and notice the way the grammar and punctuation point the last rhyming word.

The verse form adopted by Molière was considered to be classical in 17th-century France: it was how drama was written and was what the audience expected. It is inevitable that in a modern English translation we encounter some snags. We do not have a classical verse form in which our drama is written today. Translators must decide how to solve this problem. Many translators decide to modernise Molière considerably, but as a result, Molière's language is somewhat cheapened and we are not made aware of its intricacies. Directors are therefore forced to look beyond the language of the play for its craft and drama.

Modern translations

Think about...

Imagine translating *Hamlet* into French: would you choose to use the 'classical' Alexandrine or a more popular, demotic French for a modern audience?

Further reading

Tartuffe by Molière, translated by Martin Sorrell (Nick Hern Books 2002).

Martin Sorrell's translation of the play is a good one. While he uses free verse, the occasional rhymes break up and intensify certain moments. His lines are much shorter than in Molière's original. He uses a strict rhyme scheme for the final denouement speech, emphasising its artificiality.

His translation of those opening lines is as follows:

> **Madame Pernelle:** Flipote, let's go.
>
> I want to see the end of this mad family.
>
> **Elmire:** Slow down, we can't keep up with you.
>
> **Madame Pernelle:** Good – I've had enough of your 'concern'.
>
> **Elmire:** We only want to do what's best.
>
> Why the tearing hurry?

This modern version simplifies the language and gives it a new degree of informality, changing the dramatic effect of the play somewhat and lessening its seriousness.

Translations such as Sorrell's, which from the very start give it a lighter tone, make it appear strange that the play should have been controversial when it was first performed.

Another recent, successful version of the play is by Roger McGough. It is called an 'adaptation' on the cover, and rightly so. McGough writes in a demotic rhyme which plays with doggerel and he also introduces other material to the play, especially running gags (for instance, Dorine's repeated mispronunciation of Tartuffe's name, the repeated motif of badly 'translated' English proverbs and so on). This heightens the pantomime quality of the play considerably.

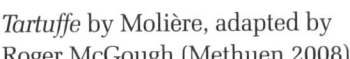

Further reading

Tartuffe by Molière, adapted by Roger McGough (Methuen 2008).

McGough's opening, after a long stage direction which does not appear in the original, is as follows:

> **Madame Pernelle:** Flipote! Where is that girl? Flipote!
>
> *Her shouting gains their attention.*
>
> Fetch the bags. This place is drivin' one mad, Flipote.
>
> To stay another day we will not.
>
> **Elmire:** But mother, why the unseemly haste?
>
> **Madame Pernelle:** Because we feel displaced.

> **Elmire:** One is obviously in the way. One is bored.
>
> No one cares about one. One is ignored.
>
> Compared to this house, Bedlam's an oasis.
>
> A mad house, that's what this place is.

This passage is witty and well contrived. Madame Pernelle's use of the impersonal 'one' in this stereotypical way is an audience pleaser and the inversions which make the rhymes work have a comedy to them. Elmire's use of the word 'unseemly' pulls the register all over the place and confirms that we are in an unreal, comic world. However, while it's effective and works a treat on stage, is it Molière? Probably not.

While we lose some of the sophistication of the original when reading the play in an English translation, it is nevertheless easier to see that the appeal of the play lies in its pantomime humour and exaggerated characters. This is the world of the commedia dell'arte.

Commedia dell'arte

The commedia dell'arte was an Italian dramatic art form whose heyday was in the 16th and 17th centuries. It was characterised by improvisation, within broadly developed plots and themes. While *Tartuffe* is not an example of the commedia, it uses the dramatic language of the form to bring substance to its plot and characters.

> Knowledge about commedia dell'arte may shape your decisions about how to stage the play – in terms of the set designs and costumes you use – and how actors might approach their parts – with gestural humour and comic exaggeration, for example.

The plot of *Tartuffe* is characteristic of the commedia material. The idea of a trickster – in our case, Tartuffe himself – is a common motif, as are the love intrigues in which he is involved, namely the interruption of a love between two young people and the seduction of his friend's wife. In *Tartuffe*, as often in commedia, servants have a bigger hand in developing the plot than their social status might be expected to allow.

Commedia dell'arte used **stock characters**, which actors specialised in the depiction of. These characters included:

> Molière had visited Italy and shared the stage with a commedia troupe.

- **Pantalone**, greedy and lecherous; the victim of practical jokes and often deceived by his wife

- The **Doctor**, a conceited man who brags of his learning

- The macho **Captain** whose actions fail to match the bravura of his speeches

- **Columbine**, the canny maidservant

- A beautiful heroine, more victim than perpetrator.

While some critics have gone to great lengths to trace exactly what each character in Molière's play owes to the characters in the commedia, this isn't really the point. It is obvious at a glance that the characters in *Tartuffe* represent a version of the Italian

Web link

There is a helpful website about the commedia here: www.theatredatabase.com/16th_century/commedia_dell_arte_001.html

> **Think about...**
>
> How could masks be used in a production of *Tartuffe*? What could they contribute to characterisation? Remember that a mask is static; although it cannot be used to convey subtle character shifts, it can be used to mock society through stereotypes and comedy. Is this suited to *Tartuffe*?

> Shakespeare complains about *lazzi* in *Hamlet*. In Act 3 scene 3, Hamlet nags the visiting players about the ways in which plays are presented: 'And let those that play your clowns speak no more than is set down for them; for there be of them that will themselves laugh, to set on some quantity of barren spectators to laugh too.'

commedia models. They, too, are stereotypical, play for laughs in a physical way through gesture and voice, and lack the deep emotional development we might expect in a play of a different genre.

In the commedia, each character was identified by his or her **mask** (though in practice not all characters wore them). These had distinctive designs for each role and have survived, more or less intact, in the masks traditionally worn at the Venice carnival.

Another significant aspect of the commedia were the ***lazzi***. These were comic interruptions to the story, inserted by actors to demonstrate their own jokes, or skills as acrobats or physical comics. Sometimes these additions were obscene or titillating. As a director of *Tartuffe*, you may want to include examples of *lazzi*. Many scenes provide the potential for them – the scene with Orgon beneath the table, for instance, or the business involving Loyal the Norman bailiff.

Setting

The commedia derived from an outdoor tradition and the plays lacked set and scenery. It seems, too, that *Tartuffe* – whose performance history was interrupted by censure and controversy – was premiered for the King in a garden. A director may wish to work with his designer to reflect something of this, even if the play is going to be performed in a conventional theatre. The set may reflect not so much the world of Tartuffe and Orgon as the world of the Sun King: garden ornaments and sculpture, perhaps. The stage might also include members of the courtly audience with whom some *lazzi* are developed. However, note that in the text, the scene divisions do not represent changes of place so much as changes of conversation.

Denouement

The tradition of the commedia gradually became part of established theatre, but its origins remained in 'outsider theatre'; the companies typically mocked high society and took risks with their performances. Again, we can see the links with *Tartuffe* which also flirts with danger in its mockery of Puritan hypocrisy. Its denouement is consistent with this mockery. Just as the situation seems impossible for Orgon, even though we know that it's almost time for the play to end, a messenger arrives, who in a long, ornate speech explains how the King knows everything, has been following Tartuffe's scandals and is returning everything to normal. This absurdly comic resolution is of course consistent with commedia-style clowning.

> **Further reading**
>
> *Commedia dell'arte: An Actor's Handbook* by John Rudlin (Routledge 1994). *Commedia dell'arte: A Handbook for Troupes* by John Rudlin and Oliver Crick (Routledge 2001).

> The ending may also have been an attempt to flatter the King, Molière's patron.

However, this kind of ending also occurs in some classical dramas, where it is called *deus ex machina* ('a god from a machine'); evidently, some crane or other was suspended over the stage or performing area and an actor playing the part of a god gave a speech which similarly put things suddenly and unequivocally to rights. Molière's use of this device suggests a nice mockery of past dramas – on the one hand scorning the clumsiness of the device and on the other, by using it himself, placing his own drama within this classical tradition.

Staging the play: key moments

By examining three key moments in more detail, we can chart the dramatic patterns of the play and identify sections which would make excellent starting points for rehearsal and further exploration of the text.

The opening

Our understanding of the debt which *Tartuffe* owes the commedia will affect the way we read and stage the play. For instance, the opening needs to establish the comic tone clearly. Madame Pernelle's scolding of the younger members of the family can be seen as less a set-up for what is to follow, and more a comic mockery of the ways in which the older generation scold and nag their juniors. There is definite scope for presenting Madame Pernelle as a kind of pantomime dame; a director needs to judge this astutely and with a certain degree of subtlety.

In his adaptation (Methuen 2008), Roger McGough suggests something of this kind:

> *Elmire, Damis, Cléante and Damis enter, engaged in loud conversation, voices raised to compete against background music. When Mme Pernelle bustles on she is ignored and unable to attract anybody's attention, shouts to her maid offstage.*

In this stage direction, we can see just how much extra material has been introduced into the production (which was originally directed by Gemma Bodinetz at the Liverpool Everyman and Playhouse in 2008): music, apparently unscripted dialogue and so on. We can also see that Madame Pernelle's character and her relationship with her family are communicated through the fact that she is ignored; this helps explain the list of grievances she is about to launch into.

Act 3 scene 2

In the first scene of the play, among the many other opinions she dispenses, Madame Pernelle has something to say about Tartuffe:

> He's a thoroughly good man.
>
> You should show him respect. I won't have
>
> Hotheads like you trying to do him down.

> This quotation and all following extracts from the play are taken from Martin Sorrell's translation of *Tartuffe* (Nick Hern Books 2002).

Molière's great trick is to build up, over two acts, a picture of Tartuffe in the audience's minds before they actually see him. The picture relayed is mainly negative, of course. Shortly after Madame Pernelle tells us that he is a 'thoroughly good man', Dorine tells the audience:

> It's a scandal how this nobody's
>
> Taken us over. When he first arrived,
>
> He looked worse than a scarecrow.
>
> He didn't even boast a pair of shoes.
>
> Now, he's so puffed up he thinks he can dictate
>
> How everyone should behave in this house

As both audience and reader, it is difficult to get rid of the image of a poor man looking 'worse than a scarecrow'. Of course, when Tartuffe finally makes his appearance, he is far from a scarecrow. The desired impact is to show that Tartuffe has all the airs and graces of the nobility, but with a puritanical set of beliefs underlying them.

Tartuffe's first appearance is at the beginning of Act 3 scene 2. Significantly, he begins by giving commands: 'Laurent, put my hair-shirt away and my scourge away.' An immediate contrast is created between the well-dressed, well-fed figure on stage and his references to self punishment and abnegation.

> The name 'Tartuffe' carries with it connotations of wealth and fine living: it echoes the Italian word for 'truffle' and also suggests the bulbous nose of a drinker.

Tartuffe goes on to find fault with Dorine's dress, offering her his handkerchief to 'cover that bosom'. Every detail of this exchange is significant; it conveys Tartuffe's rudeness and arrogance, of course, but the handkerchief in itself is also significant. In this period, the handkerchief was seen as an object of luxury and refined taste – a symbol for polite society. Here, it is juxtaposed with Tartuffe's behaviour to indicate the central hypocrisy of his character and beliefs. It is Tartuffe, of course, who draws our attention to Dorine's bosom, suggesting that he too has paid it significant attention beforehand. Finally, of course, this episode gives us an insight into how we might costume the play. We could base almost everything we design on the details we are given here: servants in low-cut dresses, men with handkerchiefs, and so on.

> **Think about...**
>
> Could you devise a *lazzo* based around this scene?

Act 5 scene 4

Loyal the Norman bailiff represents the depths to which the family has fallen at the hands of Tartuffe: he is going to throw them out onto the street. But Molière knows that he cannot afford to allow the play to become either too serious or sentimental at this point. Therefore, Loyal must deliver this crushing blow in the most comic way possible – which is, to play the content of his message against its style. Reading through Loyal's speeches in Act 5 scene 4, we get a real sense of where the comedy lies in Molière's writing:

> Such a style of delivery is, after all, a mainstay of comedy even today.

> But, first thing tomorrow morning,
>
> Be ready to clear out everything.
>
> My men will help you; I specially chose

> Big, strapping lads for the task.
>
> I think I'm being very fair.
>
> I'd ask you to do the same, Monsieur;
>
> Let us get on with our job.

The combination of superficially reasonable language and subtle threats – the 'big, strapping lads' – intensifies the kind of hypocrisy with which Tartuffe has become associated (Loyal is, here, acting as an agent of Tartuffe's). By rehearsing and exploring the rhythms and tones of Loyal's speeches, we can learn a great deal about the rhythms and tones of the play as a whole.

Questions and topics to think about

- What does the play have to say about gender roles?

- Commedia dell'arte used masks. Investigate this aspect of the commedia and consider how useful masking might be in a design concept for *Tartuffe*.

- How would a director and designer use costume to enhance the impact of the play?

- What style of stage might a director choose for this play, and why?

- Which speech would you, as a director, choose as an audition piece for each of the main characters, and why? How, as an actor, would you prepare for such an audition?

- Draw up a list of technical terms which are needed for an in-depth discussion of the play and its commedia dell'arte antecedents.

- As a director, what ideas would you have for a creative overview of the play? Which aspects of the text would you draw upon?

Questions you might expect in the exam

- As an actor, how would you perform the part of Tartuffe – referring in detail to two or three episodes in the play – in order to create comedy for an audience?

- What problems does a set designer have to solve in preparing a production of *Tartuffe*? Consider how your ideas for set design would work in practice at specific moments.

- In which scene of the play might a director or an actor find the greatest problems in realising the play? Explain what these problems are and suggest practical solutions.

Wertenbaker's play is based on Thomas Keneally's novel, *The Playmaker*, which tells the story of the first Western drama performed in Australia, Farquhar's *The Recruiting Officer*. See pages 84–91 for more information on *Our Country's Good*.

The Recruiting Officer

Introduction to the play

The Recruiting Officer (1706) has gained a lot of attention of late. Much of this is owing to a revival directed by Max Stafford-Clark at the Royal Court in 1988. This revival was played in tandem with a production of a new play, *Our Country's Good*, by Timberlake Wertenbaker, which used the same cast.

Restoration comedy

Further reading

Have a look at the following guides to Restoration comedy: *Acting in Restoration Comedy* by Simon Callow (Applause Theatre Book Publishers 1996), *Restoration Comedy in Performance* by J. L. Styan (Cambridge University Press 2008) and *The Cambridge Companion to English Restoration Theatre* by Deborah Payne Fisk (Cambridge University Press 2000).

The play is an example of the tradition we now term 'Restoration comedy' and, indeed, it is one of the last plays written in this style. Restoration comedies provided an antidote to the puritanism of Cromwell's Commonwealth. They flaunted and even celebrated amoral behaviour, especially in the character of the **rake** – the attractive, womanising young man who often provided the lead role. The plays' treatment of sexual relationships was often racy and explicit, and gained the playhouses notoriety. The audiences appear to have included the whole gamut of English society, from royalty – King Charles II was an enthusiastic supporter of comedy theatre – to the servants and workers of London.

Restoration comedies also employed the first professional **female actors** (there were no women on the Shakespearean stage, as far as we know) and their presence on stage added to the appeal and sexual frisson of performances. It became a convention of Restoration comedy for female characters to disguise themselves as men and wear men's clothes. These parts were termed 'breeches roles'; they seem to have been popular not only because they provided women with relatively significant and liberated roles, but also because they allowed women to appear in men's clothes which revealed their bodies, normally concealed by long skirts.

Political context

Charles II died in 1685, to be succeeded on the throne by his younger brother James II. James was sympathetic to Catholic causes; he was deposed by Protestant leaders in 1688 and replaced by a Protestant monarch with a tenuous claim to the throne – William of Orange, who married Mary Stuart, who had a stronger claim. This 'Glorious Revolution' was accepted relatively easily in England but much less so in Scotland and Ireland. The Battle of the Boyne in 1690 marked the defeat of Catholic Stuarts in Ireland and the victory of William of Orange.

Orangemen in Northern Ireland still mark the date of the Battle of the Boyne, on 12 July.

The playwright

George Farquhar was born in Derry, Northern Ireland, around 1677, and it seems he took part in the Battle of the Boyne as a volunteer. He studied at Trinity College, Dublin, but gave up his studies to work in the theatre. He was not a gifted performer and following a mishap in an onstage duel, during which he inadvertently injured a colleague, he gave up acting and began writing instead.

Further study

Visit the Georgian Theatre Royal in Richmond, Yorkshire (www.georgiantheatreroyal.co.uk). It was opened originally in 1788, so it is a little later than our play, but it nevertheless provides helpful insights into 18th-century English drama.

As a playwright, Farquhar had a series of minor successes, among them *The Beaux' Stratagem* (1707), but he did not make much money from them. *The Recruiting Officer* was received extremely well, however, at The Theatre Royal, Drury Lane. Farquhar died only a matter of weeks after its opening, probably of tuberculosis.

The Recruiting Officer contains many parallels with Farquhar's own life. In 1704, Farquhar joined the army as a Lieutenant of Grenadiers and was given a recruitment job in the Midlands. After a period in Lichfield, Staffordshire, he worked in Shrewsbury as a recruiting officer. Many of the references in the play, for example to public houses and businesses, seem to be to contemporary businesses in the town. Farquhar apparently wrote the play in a room of the Raven Inn (now demolished). John Ross, in his introduction to the play, quotes from an account, dating from 1765, of a woman who was able to remember the Shrewsbury of Farquhar's day and who could give historical parallels for many of his characters. Captain Plume, she says, is Farquhar himself, Mr Worthy 'is Mr Iwen of Rusason' and Justice Balance is 'Mr Berkley then Deputy Recorder of the town'.

When rehearsing his production of the play, Max Stafford-Clark took his company to Shrewsbury. This was no idle gesture: Stafford-Clark was trying to reach back to the historical origins of the play.

Further reading

See the introduction to *The Recruiting Officer* edited by John Ross (Methuen 1991).

The play has a complex set of interweaving narratives. It can be hard, even as a member of the audience, to gain a clear sense of the stories in all their detail. Try the exercise below to help you clarify the various narrative threads in the play.

Plot complexities

Allocate all the parts among your group. Having studied the text carefully, you should try to tell the story of the play from *your* character's point of view (some of the stories will, of course, have taken place off stage).

In *Letters to George*, Stafford-Clark imposes a Stanislavski-style method on rehearsals. He asks, for example, what characters' **superobjectives** are. For instance: 'Plume's is to have a good time and Kite's is probably to make as much money as possible.' In other scenes he talks openly of **objectives**. However, this use of Stanislavski-style language, though helpful, might seem inappropriate. *The Recruiting Officer* does not provide the kind of precisely observed social drama we find in Chekhov or in the work of English Edwardian playwrights. For many, Farquhar's play makes more sense as a series of comic episodes.

Further reading

Letters to George by Max Stafford-Clark (Nick Hern Books 1997).

The Recruiting Officer relies as much on **character** and **episode** as on story. In rehearsing the play, focus on how each scene works on its own terms and how each character is developed within that scene. Stafford-Clark confesses to cutting and revising scenes, particularly towards the end of the play when Farquhar's imagination is running wild. He complains, for example, that the fortune-telling scene is 'a comic excursion that is in danger of becoming disconnected from the main story'.

Further reading

Contemporary novels, such as Henry Fielding's *Tom Jones* (1749) take exactly the same approach, preferring comic episode over structural coherence.

Seduction

> **Further study**
>
> It is useful to have a clear visual image of each character before rehearsing a scene. One way to achieve this is to research 17th-century portraiture where we may find likenesses of our key characters. Many of the celebrated portraitists of the 17th century were Dutch (as was the king, William III) and included such painters as Rembrandt, Frans Hals and Caspar Netscher.

One of the linking themes in the play is **seduction**, in a very broad sense; the soldiers want to seduce both Shrewsbury's women into their beds *and* Shrewsbury's men into their army. The technique they use in both cases is similar: a display of flashy wealth with the promise of more to come in the future. While the actual consequences of such seduction are not attractive – unwanted pregnancies and death in battle – these are played down as much by Farquhar as by his characters. Plume even has a dodge which allows him to combine the two acts of seduction into one piece of harmony: 'The women, you know, are the loadstones everywhere … kiss the prettiest country wenches and you are sure of listing the lustiest fellows.' Nearly every scene can be interpreted as a seduction and in rehearsal it does well to determine who is seducing whom and why.

Many folk songs sung today have their origins in the 18th century and reveal the same world of seduction and soldiery as described in *The Recruiting Officer*. Try to listen to a selection of the following songs, all of which are available to download from iTunes. Most of them are recordings from the English folk song revival of the 1960s and 1970s and shed light on the lives of ordinary men and women in Farquhar's day.

Song	Topic
Higher Germanie by Shirley Collins	Life of a soldier
The Bird in the Bush by Shirley Collins	Seduction
The Gallant Hussar by Shirley Collins	Falling in love with a soldier
Short Jacket and White Trousers by Shirley Collins	Woman cross-dressing to seek company of a military man
Cold Haily Windy Night by Steeleye Span	A soldier seduces a virgin
O'er the Hills by Martin Carthy	This song features in the play itself, in Act 2 scene 3. It is unclear whether Farquhar is inserting a song with which he is familiar or composing one which went on to have a life of its own. It was quite normal at the time to write new words for an old tune
Gentleman Soldier by Martin Carthy with Dave Swarbrick	Bigamy and seduction – again!

Song	Topic
Fighting for Strangers by Steeleye Span	A recruiting sergeant song
The Recruiting Sergeant by The Pogues	An Irish take on the Pressing of Men

Staging the play: key moments

By examining three key moments in more detail, we can chart the dramatic patterns of the play and identify sections which would make excellent starting points for rehearsal and further exploration of the text.

The Recruiting Officer has a theatrical opening which works very well in practice. The drummer opens the play as Kite takes his place. Should he be standing on a barrel or a raised area? Kite's opening speech involves the audience in the play's action right from the start.

What costume should Kite be wearing? Historians disagree about whether soldiers wore a uniform during this period. We ought, however, to remember that we are seeking *theatrical* truths here, rather than historical ones. To make Sergeant Kite instantly recognisable as a soldier we might therefore decide to clothe him in a stroud-scarlet uniform.

Kite displays a splendid, homespun kind of rhetoric here and he successfully gains the interest of his listeners. Their apprehension at the kind of tricks that might be employed (for instance, if they try on a hat, does that mean that they have joined up?) helps the audience to see the context of this kind of recruitment; it also draws a parallel with the seduction of women later on in the play.

With the entry of Plume, the volume on stage is reduced somewhat and the relationships between the characters become the main focus. Soon they are talking about Molly and her new-born son. Plume's solution – that she marry Kite – is comic, of course, which is exacerbated further by Kite's list of wives.

By now, the basic flavour of the play has been established. In the world of Restoration comedy, Plume's relationship with Molly merely confirms his rake status rather than deem him an unsuitable match for Silvia. A well-managed opening will create this world vividly for a 21st-century audience.

Many of the folksongs of the 18th century describe women dressing as men to follow their lovers into the navy or army. And as we have heard, Restoration audiences loved the thrill of seeing an actress in men's clothes. So it should come as no surprise that Farquhar uses the device of cross-dressing in his play.

The opening

Think about...

Performing the opening in a theatre space with the house lights up, to accentuate its effect.

In 2007, the Post Office issued stamps based on soldiers' uniforms (see www.royalmail.com/portal/stamps). We could base our image of Kite on the 78p stamp: grenadier at the Battle of Blenheim, albeit in an Irish regiment.

Indeed, Kite's euphemisms for death in battle become part of this seduction process.

The female soldier (Act 3 scene 2)

The episode in Act 3 scene 2 when Silvia enters 'dressed in man's apparel' is worthy of attention, as it provides an insight into the Restoration genre in general, and Farquhar's methods in particular. The quick exchanges, the rather absurd situation ('No, no, I'm Captain Plume') and the suggestion that Plume sees through the disguise all create effective comedy on stage, even if they make little progress on the story.

The fortune-telling (Act 4 scene 2)

> Begin your exploration of the play by rehearsing this scene: you will find a lot to work on here – in terms of language, themes, its gulling of the working classes and its exaggeration – which is characteristic of the play as a whole.

Some directors find fault with the fortune-telling scene because it seems to slow down the action and detracts from the love narratives which are moving towards their respective conclusions. Even Max Stafford-Clark, usually a great respecter of writer's wishes, was uncomfortable enough to make cuts. Arguably, however, Farquhar knew exactly what he was doing here. Of course, the audience is keen to see the love narratives resolved – but a pleasure deferred is a pleasure doubled! This scene also provides us with some free-standing comedy which works well in its own right, and has a flavour of the sketch show about it.

Questions and topics to think about

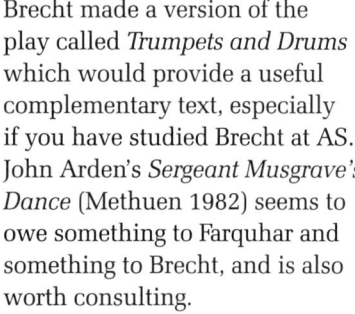

Further reading

Brecht made a version of the play called *Trumpets and Drums* which would provide a useful complementary text, especially if you have studied Brecht at AS. John Arden's *Sergeant Musgrave's Dance* (Methuen 1982) seems to owe something to Farquhar and something to Brecht, and is also worth consulting.

- What does the play have to say about gender roles?

- How might a director and designer use costume to enhance the impact of the play?

- Much of the play is set out of doors: what style of staging might a director choose for this play, and why?

- Which speech would you, as a director, choose as an audition piece for each of the main characters, and why? How, as an actor, would you prepare for such an audition?

- Draw up a list of technical terms which are needed for an in-depth discussion of the play and of Restoration comedy in general.

- What part does music play in *The Recruiting Officer* and how might it be employed or enhanced in a production?

- As a director, what ideas would you have for a creative overview of the play? Which aspects of the text would you draw upon?

Questions you might expect in the exam

- As an actor, how would you perform the part of Silvia – referring in detail to two or three episodes in the play – in order to bring out the character and to create comedy for an audience?

- What problems does a set designer have to solve in preparing a production of *The Recruiting Officer*? Consider how your ideas for set design would work in practice at specific moments.

- Sketch out and justify your casting decisions for Worthy and Brazen and then discuss how, as a director, you would work with the actors, in two or three scenes where they appear together, in order to highlight their rivalry for Melinda's love.

A Servant to Two Masters

Introduction to the play

Carlo Osvaldo Goldoni was a Venetian writer who was born in 1707. *A Servant to Two Masters* (1745) was by no means his first play. He had written, with various degrees of success, for many years, tragedies as well as comedies. Later in life, at the age of 54, he left Venice for a life in exile in Paris where he wrote his final plays in French, and where he died in 1793.

A Servant to Two Masters is a scripted version of a commedia dell'arte entertainment, and as such has a lot in common with Molière's *Tartuffe* which had a similar inspiration. Goldoni is credited with having changed the direction of Italian drama with this play. The first version was a scenario for a traditional commedia performance, but apparently Goldoni was unhappy with the liberties the actors took with his story and returned to it to produce a full script: thus, he began the movement from improvised performance to scripted drama.

To the supporters of the commedia tradition, this was a betrayal; to the guardians of bourgeois theatre, however, it was a breath of fresh air in a moribund genre. For a useful analogy to Goldoni's contribution to Italian theatre, you might like to think about George Gershwin's contribution to orchestral music. Gershwin took the largely improvisatory forms of American jazz and blues and composed orchestral music using their scales and harmonic patterns. He thereby incorporated improvisatory material into a score, which provided great impetus to the development of 20th-century art music.

In the 1990s, one of the most successful and innovative comedy programmes on British TV was *The Fast Show*. The programme's worth watching for an insight into how commedia dell'arte worked. Although *The Fast Show* is not an example of commedia, it provides a means of understanding how comedy in this tradition worked.

In *The Fast Show*, we are introduced to a cast of characters who appear in a series of short sketches. The sketches usually contain repeated familiar motifs and the ostentatious recital of catchphrases. The characters are exaggerations of recognisable personalities: the smug music journalist introducing jazz acts, the busybody at the local pub, the sexually intimidating staff at a men's outfitters, and so on. The comedy lies in this exaggeration and the familiarity of characters and catchphrases: an audience delights in the invention of another scene which will lead to a familiar conclusion and the pronouncement of a well-known catchphrase.

Commedia dell'arte worked in a similar way. The scenarios – for instance, the story of a twisted love affair or a comic old man who believes he can still attract a younger woman – provided a framework for established comic routines and catch phrases. Each character was an exaggeration of a familiar figure from vernacular life: the boastful soldier, the clever servant, the silly old fool. How

The playwright

Further reading

For further information about Goldoni and his work see *Playing with Gender: The Comedies of Goldoni* by Maggie Gunsberg (Maney Publishing 2002).

See pages 30-37 for more on *Tartuffe* and commedia dell'arte.

To be more precise, Goldoni moved from *largely* improvised performance to *largely* scripted drama.

Contemporary parallel

Further viewing

Get hold of a copy of *The Fast Show: The Ultimate Collection* (2 Entertain Video 2007). *The Fast Show* also has a website: www.bbc.co.uk/comedy/fastshow

Like Goldoni's plays, *The Fast Show* is not improvised, but scripted; however there is certainly, as with Goldoni, an improvisatory feel to the script.

might these similarities to *The Fast Show* influence the decisions made by a director presenting *A Servant to Two Masters* in a modern theatre? They could choose old-fashioned, flat-painted backdrops and costumes which echo the commedia or they could look for a setting that brings out the modern resonances in the play. What is crucial, however, is that they are able to create a sense of comic exaggeration which matches that contained in the text.

> Use some short sketch scripts from *The Fast Show*, to get used to this kind of comedy: the need for perfect control of the language and pace of the lines, the addition of gestures and pauses, and so on.

Goldoni's script is sharp; lines are short and quickly intercut for effect. Often, one character (frequently Truffaldino) will answer another and then immediately comment on their answer to the audience. Actors need to manage the pace of this skilfully and deliver lines with an attention to their comic rhythms rather than to the way they might be spoken in a realistic context.

What's more, actors need to be sensitive to the **registers** in which the lines are written. One of Goldoni's achievements was to combine slang, Venetian dialect and standard Italian in his plays. Modern versions in English have to simulate this rich variety of language by using a wide range of registers. Lee Hall's version is successful in combining standard language, formal language (Lombardi's absurd legalisms) and the demotic (Truffaldino's swearing).

Harlequin

> Harlequin's costume, like that of the rugby team named after him, is in two colours. Goldoni uses this idea to suggest that Truffaldino is wearing the livery of two, different masters.

Goldoni's play focuses on the role of the Harlequin. Truffaldino dominates the play and his role is characteristic of the Harlequin's role in the commedia drama. Harlequin is a character who lives on his wits; he is a clown – one of the *zanni* – who customarily neglects his job, and struggles to read and write. He is often dishonest and more interested in pursuing his own love affairs than in performing his duties. He engages in significant physical humour, and the performer was expected to improvise pratfalls and visual gags to embellish his role and to entertain the audience. Indeed, Goldoni's script contains many comic asides made by performers to the audience – again, an example of Goldoni 'fixing' in script form the ad lib banter which developed in commedia performances between clowns and the audience.

So, what kind of theatre are we dealing with here? It is not revolutionary (although it must be noted that revolutionaries in France spared Goldoni out of respect, it is said, for his depiction of the common man) and it is not unduly challenging. This is theatre which gently mocks society. We are not supposed to treat Florindo as a murderer (even though he is). We are invited to suspend our moral judgement for the sake of the story and for entertainment, and a good director will ensure that their choice of set, costume and acting style is harmonious with this. Without its sense of fun, *A Servant to Two Masters* could be said to hardly exist at all.

Staging the play: key moments

By examining three key moments in more detail, we can chart the dramatic patterns of the play and identify sections which would make excellent starting points for rehearsal and further exploration of the text.

A director must use the first few minutes of the play to establish the comic world which it inhabits firmly in the audience's mind. Without careful attention to a cohesive **style** – drawing together acting, set and costumes – the audience will receive mixed messages.

As with many comedies, there is a shadow of tragedy here: The betrothal is conducted with a certain solemnity; we hear that a former fiancé has met 'such a dreadful demise in Turin'; an interruption brings a premature end to Silvio and Clarice's happiness. However, Goldoni provides plenty of material for a director to steer away from these tragic elements. Firstly, the language is wonderfully absurd – it certainly is in Lee Hall's modern English version. On the first page of the play, the solemnity of the betrothal is punctured by language in the 'wrong' register. Dr Lombardi – who later delivers speeches full of cod learning – responds in very casual language to the betrothal: 'Excellent, that's all sorted then. No turning back now.' The servant Smeraldina changes the mood still further by commenting in demotic language: 'The lucky cow.' By page 2, the audience should feel that they are watching something which is as far removed from tragedy as a pantomime is: 'He was run through by the girl's lover and that, I'm afraid, was that,' says Pantaloon. 'In Turin?' he's asked. 'In the very middle,' he replies, with comic ambiguity .

Truffaldino's entrance – notwithstanding the complexities of plot which this initiates – is truly comic and provides an actor ample opportunity to embellish his part with visual and improvised action. Lee Hall's version even provides a reference to the famous *Monty Python* Dead Parrot sketch:

Pantaloon:	The man's out of his mind. Federigo Rasponi is dead.
Truffaldino:	Dead?
Pantaloon:	Dead. Defunct. Deceased. Demised. Kaput. No more, sir.

In the opening scenes, Truffaldino's harlequin humour remains largely verbal. However, in Act 2 scene 12 we find a good example of the visual and physical comedy we would expect from a harlequin role. This scene provides an excellent way of beginning your study of *A Servant to Two Masters*. By perfecting the rhythm, the action and the nonsense of this meal, which is served chaotically to two tables by a hungry servant, you will come close to an understanding of the basic principles underlying Goldoni's method and intentions.

Directing such a scene requires a huge amount of cooperation from everyone. It is a scene dominated by Truffaldino, of course, but without the perfect cooperation of the actors playing the waiters and the stage management team offstage, the scene will fail. It is full of opportunities for the kind of embellishments one might expect from the commedia.

The opening

Further reading

All quotations are from Lee Hall's adaptation of the play (Methuen 1999).

Further viewing

You can view the Dead Parrot sketch on YouTube: www.youtube.com

Think about...

How should Truffaldino respond to each of Pantaloon's words?

The dinner (Act 2 scene 12)

A lot can be learned about a play by reading reviews of successful productions. This is what Lizzie Loveridge says about the first modern production, in London, of Lee Hall's version, which he prepared for the Young Vic and the RSC:

> Robert Innes Hopkins's wooden set, painted in terracotta and yellow, turquoise and green, uses the traverse stage to good effect for this physical and energetic comedy. At either end of the long thin stage, which bisects the audience, the archways are transformed with a change of doors or railings or curtains to shift the scene from park to palazzo to inn. ... The hotel has two doors for our servant to race in and out of in his attempt to serve a meal to each master simultaneously.
>
> I particularly liked the chaotic meal scene in Brighella's hotel in which three cast members double up as a trio of comic waiters who briskly try to get on with their work while Truffaldino intercepts the food. Much is made of the innuendo of a grisly named suet pudding with currants, Spotted Dick, and Truffaldino, ever hungry ends up eating for two, flinging rissoles into the audience and dunking his whole head in the ragout.

Web link

This review can be read in full at: www.curtainup.com/servantand2masters.html

These two paragraphs encapsulate all that we have understood about the play: the need for an appropriate set to establish the right image from the start, its physical humour, and the importance of engaging with the audience. Getting the meal scene right establishes the rules for the rest of the play.

The end

Lee Hall's version provides Truffaldino with a marvellous speech at the end of the play. He responds to Florindo's insult – rendered by Hall as 'You deceitful little arse' – with a justification for his chaos. It has all been, he says in a splendidly anachronistic phrase, 'a miracle of time management'. While he seems to be speaking up for the working man, we know not to take anything he says at face value; though he accepts that there were some 'complications' (which nearly led to a double suicide) he maintains that 'it's all worked out pretty well'.

Truffaldino then turns to the audience and in a final rhyming couplet bids us all 'good night'. Once again, we are given a clear insight into the comic world which Goldoni created. While the language may have changed in the translation and the audience have changed in the course of time, the comic spirit of the commedia seems to have survived intact in the play.

Questions and topics to think about

➤ What does the play have to say about gender roles?

➤ The commedia used masks. Investigate this part of its tradition and consider how useful masking might be in a design concept for *A Servant to Two Masters*. Bear in mind that it is a quick-witted play, so you may need to use half-masks or designs which make speech easy and clearly audible.

➢ How would a director and designer combine costume and set to enhance the impact of the play? Look at contemporary paintings of commedia troupes.

➢ Much commedia performance was out of doors. What style of stage might a director choose for *A Servant to Two Masters*, and why?

➢ Draw up a list of technical terms which are needed for an in-depth discussion of the play and its commedia dell'arte antecedents.

➢ Which speech would you, as a director, choose as an audition piece for each of the main characters, and why? How, as an actor, would you prepare for such an audition?

➢ As a director, what ideas would you have for a creative overview of the play? What aspects of the text would you draw upon?

Questions you might expect in the exam

➢ As an actor, how would you perform the part of Pantaloon – referring in detail to two or three episodes in the play – in order to create comedy for an audience?

➢ What problems does a set designer have to solve in preparing a production of *A Servant to Two Masters*? Consider how your ideas for set design would work in practice at specific moments.

➢ Think about the effects you, as a director, would want to create in staging the relationship between Silvio and Clarice. Outline your casting decisions for the pair and discuss how you would direct them in at least two episodes where they appear together.

The Seagull

Introduction to the play

Chekhov's plays are highly distinctive and original, and their influence upon European drama throughout the 20th century has been enormous. However, it's useful to consider the extent to which the subject matter and methods of 19th-century European novels impacted on the playwright's work.

19th-century novels

Broadly speaking, 19th-century novels deal with big ideas concerning society, its morality and values, the function of art and the role of the artist. They tend to use a broad cast of characters, who grow old and change as the narrative progresses. They often have a strong sense of place and setting, using the weather to intensify the emotional impact of scenes. Nineteenth-century novelists – in England, we might think of the Brontë sisters, George Eliot and Thomas Hardy – preferred, by and large, to show rather than to tell. This is one reason why their novels lend themselves particularly well to cinematic or television adaptation: the reader is invited to watch and interpret key scenes, rather than held at arm's length and told about them.

Further reading

Chekhov was also a short story writer. Given the subject matter of the play, you might want to read some of these; see *Forty Stories* by Anton Chekhov (Vintage 2002). You might also like to read *Selected Short Stories* by Virginia Woolf (Penguin 2000) – keen students will notice the debt she owes Chekhov.

Chekhov's plays are relatively long, but their scope is longer. The stories they tell are often long and complex. Each character has a slightly different take on events. Like a novelist, Chekhov invites his audience to attend closely to subtle characterisation as he shows a handful of key scenes in the development of a series of linked personal stories.

Stanislavski

It is hard to discuss Chekhov's work as a dramatist without mentioning Stanislavski. Stanislavski realised that in order to perform Chekhov 'truthfully', a director and their cast needed to tease out the subtle narratives in Chekhov's dialogues. Some material is explicit – Stanislavski called this 'the given circumstances' – but much is implicit and unspoken, voiced only as subtext or discovered only as an explanation for otherwise unmotivated acts. Stanislavski found it valuable to talk about characters' **objectives**, exploring what each character wants from a situation and how they act in order to achieve it.

Further reading

See *AQA AS Drama Study Guide* (Rhinegold 2008) for a detailed analysis of Stanislavski's work. You may also like to look at *Stanislavski: An Introduction* by Jean Benedetti (Methuen 1982).

This technique remains today the best way to appreciate the density of Chekhov's imagination and his writing. No student can really work on *The Seagull* without a study of Stanislavski's practice.

The Seagull draws heavily upon Chekhov's own life and experiences. The play dates from 1896. By then, Chekhov, who was born in 1860, had left home for Moscow, written both unsuccessful and successful plays, graduated as a doctor, worked among peasant communities in the Russian countryside, written short stories for magazines and bought a farm 50 miles outside Moscow. This biographical knowledge should help a director and cast to appreciate how much detail Chekhov invested in his characters.

Rehearse a character's part by 'cutting out' their individual speeches from the play and then editing them together into one long monologue. This will require some cutting and editing, of course, to achieve fluency and clarity, but the effect can be astonishing. Chekhov's most successful plays can be seen to operate as a series of interrupted monologues.

Performance history

The first performance of the play in Saint Petersburg in 1896 was not a great success. While we can now appreciate that Chekhov was trying something new and experimental in *The Seagull*, the first production used conventional, 19th-century performance techniques. It would have been customary at the time for actors only to have a rudimentary knowledge of the play, to have rehearsed it lightly, and to rely on their own costumes and the prompter considerably more than we would expect today. As a result, the subtleties of the play remained undeveloped, and the audience found Treplev's suicide attempt in Act 4 farcical and the stuffed seagull absurd.

Further reading

J. L. Styan provides an excellent account of the performance history of *The Seagull* in *Modern Drama in Theory and Practice 1: Realism and Naturalism* (Cambridge University Press 1981).

The founders of the Moscow Art Theatre – Nemirovitch-Danchenko and Stanislavski – were able to see something more in the play, however, and prepared another production of the play in 1898. As J. L. Styan explains, Stanislavski's company gave the play 26 rehearsals. Time was spent in perfecting subtle gestures and the 'elusive tone' of each scene. Stanislavski paid enormous attention, too, to the sets and sound effects.

When exploring *The Seagull*, it is important to understand the distinction between metonymy and metaphor.

Metonymy is the name given to the technique whereby a whole is suggested by describing a part. We build an impression of a whole house by seeing key details of just one room; we understand a character by seeing how they respond to just one or two key situations; we grasp a relationship through two or three snatches of dialogue. The task for Stanislavski and his company was to unpick the metonymic elements of the play: establish the whole from the parts which Chekhov revealed in the text.

Chekhov himself provides us with the clearest explanation of metonymy in a long speech in the *The Seagull*, in which the emotionally drained and desperate Treplev is considering his work. Just as he has lost Nina to his rival writer, so he finds that he lacks the other's instinctive gifts of composition. He looks at a passage of his own writing:

> The description of the moonlit evening is long and forced. Trigorin's worked out his methods, it's easy enough for him. He gives you the neck of a broken bottle glittering against a weir and the black shadow of a mill-wheel – and there's your moonlit night all cut and dried.

This passage can be understood as Chekhov's defence of his own literary style. He is saying: you won't get long, sententious, sentimental detail here, but you will, as a director, actor and audience, get puzzles to solve, which can be far more satisfying.

On the other hand, Chekhov is not afraid to add **metaphor** to his basic diet of metonymy, in order to illustrate complex themes and ideas. The dog which howls all night certainly gives local colour and an insight into Shamrayev's rather antisocial personality, but does it represent anything else? Are Treplev and Trigorin, with their plays and stories, any more than 'dogs which howl in the night'? And what about the seagull motif? The seagull is drawn to the lake, which is both its desire and the scene of its death. What relation does this bear to the relationships in the play?

Staging the play: key moments

By examining three key moments in more detail, we can chart the dramatic patterns of the play and identify sections which would make excellent starting points for rehearsal and further exploration of the text.

Metonymy and metaphor

> Many 19th-century novels rely heavily on metonymy; this enhances their overall 'realistic' nature as in reality this is the way by which we come to terms with the world: we infer wholes from glimpses of parts.

Further reading

All quotes from *The Seagull* are from *Five Plays* by Anton Chekhov, translated and introduced by Ronald Hingley (Oxford World's Classics 1998).

The opening

Think about...

The opening description of the scene ('The scene is laid in the park on Sorin's estate...') dates from a time when flat, painted sets were the norm. However, a modern audience, used to cinema and advanced theatrical technology, may treat a painted flat with surprise. A director should try to translate Chekhov's described scene into something which will work in the contemporary theatre. How could we suggest rural, Russian setting which is both claustrophobic and open? How could we convey that 'the sun has just set'?

There are few easy solutions provided on the first page of the text, and plenty of problems – all of which have to be solved by the director and cast.

Many critics use the term **realism** when writing about Chekhov; sometimes the rather specialist term 'naturalism' is also used, as if it were a synonym. Yet the opening page of *The Seagull* shows us immediately quite how *unrealistic* Chekhov's work can be. Psychologically, it's realistic, of course: the characters have convincing motivations, and develop in intriguing and credible ways. However, 'realistic' is perhaps too bland a term to describe the play: the set is far too complex to be wholly realistic, and the speeches made by characters are longer than any we'd encounter in normal, everyday dialogue.

Immediately, the characters embark on their 'interrupted' monologues. There is no talking about the weather here. We're straight off with: 'Why do you wear black all the time?' Medvedenko, it transpires, is hopelessly in love with Masha, who is rather cruel to him later in the play. He feels – rightly – that Masha's gloomy disposition is a rejection of his love; when he asks about her black clothes, therefore, he is trying to talk about his unrequited love for her. However, she makes this explicit before he does: 'Your loving me is all very touching...'

Act 2

Chekhov risks a lot with some of his writing. In Act 2, Treplev 'lays a seagull at [Nina's] feet'; this appears an absurd and preposterous gesture which could risk the scorn of an unsympathetic audience. Why does Treplev do such a thing? Certainly, when he looks at the dead bird and says 'I shall soon kill myself in the same way', we might feel that he is being sentimental and self-dramatising. Therefore when later we see him wounded from the attempt, in another riskily comic moment, we might be surprised that he meant what he said.

Treplev and Trigorin are rivals and in the long speeches which follow the seagull moment, first Treplev and then Trigorin open their hearts to Nina. Their motives for doing so are complex and have as much to with their relationship with one another (and their relationship with Treplev's mother) as with Nina. As we find in Act 4, in many ways Nina is the real victim of their rivalry.

When you look at these speeches, as an actor or director, you may think about delivery, about what first Treplev and then Trigorin are thinking, about what they want from this exposition of their ideas, and so on. But the really hard part in the conclusion to Act 2 is considering how to stage Nina's speeches. Her reaction to their long speeches is harder to calculate and stage effectively and, in the end, is more important.

The end

In a letter to Alexei Suvorin written in 1895, Chekhov explained that he had ended the play 'pianissimo', and 'contrary to all the rules of dramatic art'. It seems that in his production, Stanislavski included additional dramatic effects – off-stage sounds and laughter, and gestures – to make up for the offhandedness of the script, and you will need to consider how the audience ought to react to the ending. Although laughter may *seem* out of the question, the rhythms and nature of the final speeches are the rhythms of the comic, not the tragic. Indeed, if you look back to the title page you will find the play described as a 'comedy'.

The problem of whether to bring out the tragic or comic elements of the play is not easily solved. However, by tackling the three scenes discussed above – the opening, the dead seagull and the end – by preparing compilation monologues for the characters and applying some key elements of Stanislavski's approach, you will develop tools to reach your own solutions. It is these solutions – and, most importantly, your rationale for them – which you must write about in the examination.

> **Further reading**
> *A Life in Letters* by Anton Chekhov, translated by Rosamund Bartlett and Anthony Phillips (Penguin 2004).

> **Further reading**
> See *Modern Drama in Theory and Practice 1: Realism and Naturalism* by J. L. Styan (Cambridge University Press 1981).

Questions and topics to think about

- How does Chekhov's drama differ from other plays you have read?

- How might costume and set contribute to *The Seagull*?

- What problems might the designer encounter when developing the sets and props for the play?

- Consider the pace of each episode.

- Which speech would you, as a director, choose as an audition piece for each of the main characters, and why? How, as an actor, would you prepare for such an audition?

- As a director, what ideas would you have for a creative overview of the play? What aspects of the text would you draw upon?

Questions you might expect in the exam

- As an actor, how would you perform the part of Nina – referring in detail to two or three episodes in the play? What response would you expect from an audience?

- What problems does a set designer have to solve in preparing a production of *The Seagull*? Consider how your ideas for set design would work in practice at specific moments.

- Think about the effects you, as a director, would want to create in staging the relationship between Arkadina and her son Treplev. Outline your casting decisions for the pair and discuss how you would direct them in at least two episodes where they appear together to bring out the subtleties of their relationship.

Lady Windermere's Fan

Introduction to the play

Lady Windermere's Fan was Oscar Wilde's first big success on the stage. It opened on 22 February 1892 at St James's Theatre, London. Oscar Wilde received an advance on royalties of £100 – a huge sum in 1892.

> Wilde was even offered £1,000 for the copyright, a sum he sensibly declined.

The play combines characteristically Victorian sentiment with Wilde's wit, epigrams and paradoxes (some of them recycled from their use in his 1891 novel, *The Picture Of Dorian Gray*). In a 1930 introduction to the plays, Hesketh Pearson, who does not seem to be a lover of the play, says that 'The audience of those days wanted a wronged and noble woman, a sinning but repentant man, and a high moral tone. Wilde gave them what they wanted, using it all as framework for his wit; and the combination of Mayfair with morals was irresistible.'

Further reading

Plays, Prose Writings and Poems by Oscar Wilde, edited by Hesketh Pearson (Everyman Library 1930).

The playwright

Wilde was born in Dublin in 1856 into a well-off upper-middle-class family. He read classics at Trinity College, Dublin and won a scholarship to study at Magdalen College, Oxford. Pearson says: 'He took with him from Oxford a reputation as a brilliant talker, a promising poet and an incorrigible *poseur*.' In London, he was welcomed into society, wrote Romantic poetry and dressed as a dandy, leading the Aesthetic Movement whose motto was 'Art For Art's Sake'.

> The Aesthetic Movement was mocked widely, in *Punch*, for example, and famously in Gilbert and Sullivan's comic opera, *Patience* (1881).

Wilde married Constance Lloyd in 1884 and wrote several successful plays in the 1890s, including, alongside *Lady Windermere's Fan*, *A Woman of No Importance* (1893) and *The Importance of Being Earnest* (1895).

His downfall in 1895 was astonishing. Although Wilde had made many friends in London, he had also made some enemies through his sarcasm and behaviour. He began a lawsuit claiming libel against the Marquis of Queensbury but the action failed and rebounded on him, as he was arrested for 'lewd behaviour' (homosexuality) and sentenced to two years' hard labour. Upon release in 1897, his health was seriously weakened and he died three years later in a Paris hotel.

Further reading

For more information about Wilde's life and work see *Authors in Context: Oscar Wilde* by John Sloan (Oxford University Press 2003) and *The Cambridge Companion to Oscar Wilde* by Peter Raby (Cambridge University Press 1997).

Comedy of manners

Lady Windermere's Fan is a comedy of manners. It depicts the society from which its audience is drawn, the upper middle class and upper class of Victorian England. It mocks their way of behaving while at the same time reinforcing their values and prejudices. Although their values are shown as shallow and at times deplorable, the characters are presented as decorous and in many ways attractive.

Key themes

As we would expect in a comedy of manners, **social mores** are one of the play's key themes. Mrs Erlynne is outside society, for reasons which are only hinted at, and she seeks, through a hold over Lord Windermere which is not at first made clear, to re-enter society and to take her place at the soirées and balls of the wealthiest London circles.

The tension in the relationship between Lord and Lady Windermere, and Lord Darlington's flirtatious advances to Lady Windermere are played out against a comic backdrop of shallow, social behaviour. This dramatic juxtaposition draws attention to the second chief theme, that of society's **hypocrisy**. Throughout the play, sometimes wittily, sometimes severely, Wilde uses his characters to draw attention to the contradictions in Victorian values.

> Often these hypocrisies address gender issues. It seems acceptable, for instance, for the unmarried Lord Darlington to propose an elopement to Lady Windermere, however it is implied that Mrs Erlynne has been ostracised from 'polite society' for doing much the same thing a generation earlier.

Although Wilde's touch is light and his manner often cynical, the play addresses the most serious of moral issues: adultery, blackmail and divorce. Those critics who in Victorian England wrote unfavourably about the play found in this combination of light comedy and serious social satire something which was threatening and uncomfortable.

Characters

As characters, **Lady Windermere** and **Lord Windermere** are thoroughly serious, both in their language, their manner and the issues which concern them. Their relationship is under strain and they both have secrets to keep from one another: his knowledge of Mrs Erlynne's true identity and her relationship with Darlington. But they play these serious issues out against the flimsiest of backdrops: light conversation, social diaries and a birthday ball. As actors we must find ways to make both the serious and the flippant work together in dramatic harmony.

Mrs Erlynne presents the greatest conflict in the play. She wants to mingle with society – to be flippant again – but she is drawn ineluctably towards the Windermeres' seriousness. An actor must recognise the distinction between these two levels of the role and move, vocally and emotionally, between them.

Other characters in the play are subsidiary, but contribute significantly to the play's impact. Windermere and Darlington are surrounded by a group of wits and humorists – whom the audience may suspect are versions of Wilde himself – who bring to the play much of its charm. Perhaps the most comic character in the play is **Agatha**; while she only says one thing on stage – 'Yes, mamma' – she says it with such effect that she gets exactly what she wants.

Tragedy and comedy

The play combines the seriousness of a tragedy with the lightness of a comedy. We expect a comedy to end with a marriage, and this one does, with Augustus to marry Mrs Erlynne. We expect a tragedy to end with a death; while there is no death here, there is something solemn about the way in which Mrs Erlynne sacrifices her dreams of social standing for Lady Windermere's sake. Directors need to consider how best to manage the stark contrast between comic and tragic elements in the play.

Farce and melodrama

The play contains elements of both **farce** and **melodrama**. The farce is easy to spot, with Agatha and Augustus leading the way in their comic bantering. The melodramatic elements are harder to evaluate. This is largely because melodrama often gains a bad press these days and is regarded as a dead end in theatre; however in the 19th century melodramas were successful and often adventurous plays. They were popular and had the potential to carry political messages (although these were often reactionary and in favour of the status quo).

One common feature of melodrama is its use of **documents**. The plot often turns on the discovery of an important document, such as a pardon at the gallows, a will, a ticket or a passport. In *Lady Windermere's Fan*, there are three documents whose dramatic significance and importance almost exceed those of some of the characters:

1. **Lady Windermere's letter**, written for her husband but intercepted by Mrs Erlynne, is crucial. During its short life (it's put on the fire in Act 3) it dominates the stage, because it represents metaphorically the state of the Windermeres' marriage. Learning to work alongside such a powerful tool is an important task for actors.

2. Similarly, the **bank book** in Act 1 whose contents fuel Lady Windermere's suspicions, lies on the stage as an accusation to which Lord Windermere must respond.

3. Finally, the **fan** itself is a kind of document. The meaning of the fan changes as the play progresses. Lady Windermere sees in it at first a symbol of her husband's love for her. In Darlington's apartment it then becomes a symbol of adultery. At the end of the play, it becomes a symbol of repentance and reunion.

> Stanislavski used the term 'communion' to describe the way in which actors respond to one another onstage. The presence of each of these documents gives the actors an opportunity to practise this technique. Each must see in the object a different kind of symbol: the bank book is a sign for Lady Windermere of her husband's infidelity, while for him it is a sign of her distrust.

> Peter Hall's 2002 production of the play recognised the symbolic importance of the fan by incorporating a large, stylised fan into the set, designed by John Gunter.

Staging the play: key moments

The opening

By examining three key moments in more detail, we can chart the dramatic patterns of the play and identify sections which would make excellent starting points for rehearsal and further exploration of the text.

From the very start of the play, Wilde establishes a rhythm in his writing. Actors need to work on their lines, pointing them and pacing them so that the cool, calculating nature of Wilde's wit can emerge on stage.

The **setting** is established straight away. What might seem a period setting to us now was in Wilde's day a contemporary, albeit narrow, social milieu (which many of those in the audience would have inhabited themselves). The furnishings of Lord Windermere's morning room establish his class and wealth, while Lady Windermere's actions – 'arranging roses in a blue bowl' – combined with her youthful beauty confirm her place in this high-class society.

The butler, Parker, introduces an added tone of formality to the setting. He announces the arrival of Lord Darlington, whose name provokes a response in Lady Windermere. She 'hesitates a moment', and this hesitation is characteristic of the way in which her character is more serious than many others in the play. Left alone for a moment, she tells the audience, 'It's best for me to see him before tonight. I'm glad he's come.'

Think about...

Throughout the play, Wilde is assiduous in managing audience response. Here, he sets out to intrigue us. What is going on? What does Lord Darlington mean to Lady Windermere?

Wilde enjoys the characteristically English, stiff-upper-lip manner of English society. While the play is about honour and dishonour, elopement, adultery and blackmail, it is conducted in a language which is grammatically cool and precise. As a prelude to the conversation between the two, Parker's announcement – 'Lord Darlington' – establishes this world of solemn formality, which is maintained by their polite greetings.

Lady Windermere's reaction to Darlington's flirtatious comment is significant. She gives 'a short pause' before scolding him, 'you annoyed me last night.' The actors need to relish the underlying sexual tension here. They need to pace the lines exactly to reveal both their superficial meaning and their levels of subliminal emotion. Throughout the play, emotions are often concealed beneath fine expression. Indeed, the emotionally charged dialogue here is married to the business of serving tea. Everything is exact and precise: the grammar, the rhythm and the stage business of tea cups.

Lady Windermere is given few witty lines in the play; her job is to play the sentimental woman apparently wronged by a husband. Darlington, on the other hand, brings to the dialogue some of the male 'smoking-room' banter which we see more of later on. He expresses himself with a Wildean lilt and clipped rhythm:

> Oh, nowadays so many conceited people go about Society pretending to be good, that I think it shows rather a sweet and modest disposition to pretend to be bad.

Darlington alludes to the relationship between Lord Windermere and Mrs Erlynne, a relationship made explicit by the Duchess of Berwick later in the scene. This brings out from Lady Windermere an exposition of the values of the play. At this stage, she thinks morality is a matter of black and white: 'If we had these "hard and fast rules", we should find life much more simple.'

Having decided to follow Lord Darlington, Lady Windermere writes a letter to her husband. Suspecting this, after Parker's exit, Mrs Erlynne opens it. Her speech is full of melodramatic stops and starts as Wilde traces her emotional turmoil. It reaches a climax – we have already noted how rhythm is a characteristic device in Wilde's writing – when Mrs Erlynne reveals to the audience that she is Lady Windermere's mother: 'Oh, how terrible! The same words that twenty years ago I wrote to her father! and how bitterly I have been punished for it!'

Mrs Erlynne covers for her absent daughter in the dialogue with Lord Windermere. At a loss to know how to keep Windermere away until she has solved the problem, she seizes upon Augustus who appears to have proposed marriage to her. What makes this dialogue so effective is the skillful way in which the melodramatic sentimentality of Mrs Erlynne's position is counterbalanced by the farcical character of Augustus. She demands he take Windermere down to his club and keep him there for 'as long as possible', to

Think about...

A director may look for ideas here for the design of the play. Lady Windermere sees things in black and white – people who commit a fault 'should never be forgiven' – and she is called a Puritan by Darlington. It is easy to see a colour scheme emerging. The play's main action will surround an evening ball where the men will wear black and white evening dress. It may be possible to design the whole play around this observation. What colours might the women's costumes be? Would Mrs Erlynne wear a different colour?

Further study

Two or three years before Wilde's success with *Lady Windermere's Fan*, the most controversial play in London was Ibsen's *A Doll's House* (1879). This was considered shocking because of its frank depiction of the break up of a marriage. The parallels with *Lady Windermere's Fan* are intriguing. Read Ibsen's play and compare his sombre treatment and 'tragic' ending with Wilde's lightness of touch and more 'comic' conclusion.

which Augustus replies, 'but you said you wished me to keep early hours!"

The audience is manipulated beautifully and a good production will manage this easily. First, we are shocked by Mrs Erlynne's revelation, though we may have been suspecting it; we are then drawn into her anxiety for her daughter, and come to understand why Lord Windermere had been apparently so close to her; alongside all of this, Wilde still gives as a comic character to laugh at. For if the audience does not laugh at this rueful line of Augustus's, something is missing in the production. The same technique is used to finish the act. Mrs Erlynne, preoccupied about her daughter, ignores Augustus's hints about marriage, simply giving him instructions. He ends the scene alone, with the lines, delivered flatly to the audience: 'Well, really, I might be her husband already. Positively I might.' Despite everything, the act ends with laughter, which reassures the audience that the second half of the play will in some way end happily.

Darlington's rooms

There are clear elements of melodrama in the third act when the men arrive in Darlington's rooms unexpectedly, Mrs Erlynne having ambushed Lady Windermere there.

> Rehearsing this particular scene, whether you are preparing for a full production of the play or not, will help you to understand Wilde's drama and his methods.

Firstly, as the men enter, Lady Windermere hides behind a curtain, and Mrs Erlynne disappears into an adjoining room. Discovery in a man's rooms will destroy their reputations: the stakes are high. Against this, Wilde plays his strong suit, the apparently careless wit of the men. Once again, every epigram is perfectly balanced and rhythmic, reflecting the perfect dramatic balance of the scene: the serious concerns of the women and the light-hearted position of the men.

> The epigrams are delivered like a sketch from *The Fast Show*: 'Oh! Gossip is charming! History is merely gossip. But scandal is gossip made tedious by morality.' 'Now, my dear Tuppy, don't be led astray into the paths of virtue.' And so on.

But Lord Darlington's mind is clearly on other things. It is he who is given one of the most famous lines: 'No, we are all in the gutter, but some of us are looking at the stars.' The audience enjoys the wit of this and is also reminded of the two women hiding in the apartment.

In a final piece of melodrama here, it is the fan which gives the game away. Wilde's pacing is perfect. First, the fan – 'What is my wife's fan doing here in your rooms?' – then a movement behind the curtain, and finally Mrs Erlynne's entrance on which the curtain falls.

Questions and topics to think about

- What is the relationship between the play and its audience? Is the play simply meant to be entertaining?
- How might costume and set contribute to Wilde's comedy?
- What problems might the designer encounter when developing the sets and props for the play?
- Consider the pace of each conversation.

- Which speech would you, as a director, choose as an audition piece for each of the main characters, and why? How, as an actor, would you prepare for such an audition?

- As a director, what ideas would you have for a creative overview of the play? Which aspects of the text would you draw upon?

Questions you might expect in the exam

- As an actor, how would you perform the part of Lady Windermere – referring in detail to two or three episodes in the play? What response would you expect from an audience?

- What problems does a costume designer have to solve in preparing a production of *Lady Windermere's Fan*? Consider how your ideas for costume would work in practice at specific moments.

- Think about the effects you, as a director, would want to create in staging the relationship between Lady Windermere and her husband. Outline your casting decisions for the pair and discuss how you would direct them in at least two episodes where they appear together to bring out the changing nature of their relationship.

Unit 3b: The 20th Century or Contemporary Drama

Introduction

In Unit 3b, you will study a play in detail, considering it as a text for performance. You will need to consider it from the perspective of audience, actor and designer, but most importantly, from the viewpoint of director. The examination question will provide an extract from the play and you will be asked to discuss how you would stage the extract in order to bring out a valid, personal interpretation.

When writing your answer, you should be able to offer a critical overview of the entire play and provide clear directorial aims which takes into account the text's individual qualities and content, as well as its style, genre and history. The best students will demonstrate how their own research has helped them to clarify and broaden their understanding of the text, and the ways in which it can be performed. They will understand how to match directorial aims with performance techniques and design, so as to prompt an appropriate audience response. They will also be able to articulate creative ideas about how to stage the play and propose a good range of practical approaches to doing this. There will be clear links demonstrated between theoretical understanding of the play and practical suggestions for staging it.

The quality of your writing is important. Poorly expressed or clumsy work suggests poor understanding and a weakness in communication. A good director should be articulate and perceptive, and the best answers in this part of the examination will demonstrate these qualities.

> Because the examination paper will include an extract from the play, the examination board stipulates specific editions for texts in translation.

In the exam

First steps

- **Read the extract carefully.** Don't skim-read it and then start making generalisations. You will know the play well, of course, and should recognise the extract straight away. You will also have the whole text with you in the exam. Nevertheless, the extract is printed there for a reason: to emphasise the need to pay close attention to it in preparing your answer.

- **Jot down everything you know about the play which is relevant to the question.** Include not only what you know about the play theoretically, but also what you know emotionally about performing the play, from your work in class experimenting with scenes and practising rehearsal skills. Also, include what you know from having taking part in, or having watched, a production of the play.

> It is amazing how many students come out of an exam regretting not having included something important in their answers.

- **Jot down the problems which this extract might present.** Try to be as insightful as possible and work through the extract as a director would during a rehearsal. Consider, for example, the problems raised for the actors by what they have to say or do and how they have to react (it's often harder to listen to a long speech than to deliver it), and those raised for designers and stage managers. Consider, too, the problems which may be created by performing an old play in a contemporary theatre, or a foreign-language play to a British audience.

- **Jot down ideas for staging the extract.** Focus on one clear reading of the piece, but be prepared to offer several solutions to problems where this is relevant.

Once you have jotted down your ideas, you are ready to begin writing your answer.

Writing your answer

- **Place the extract in context.** Begin your answer by noting where the extract comes in the play as a whole. What has just happened? What elements of this extract will be important as the play develops? What is revealed here about important relationships? How are key themes articulated? Be careful not to tell the entire story; some mention of plot and narrative should be sufficient. You should treat this opening as if you were a director beginning a day's rehearsal: remind your cast where they are in the play.

- **Articulate your directorial aims.** Once you have briefly established a context for the extract, present a quick overview of your directorial aims for the play as a whole. In articulating these aims, you should refer now and again to the extract in front of you, but you should also be able to refer to other key episodes in the play, research you have done into the period, genre and style of the play, and performance conventions for such drama. Where relevant, you might also like to refer to the play's performance history and to other works by the same playwright. Imagine here that you are a director presenting ideas for a production to the board of a theatre company: you want to impress them with your understanding of the play and its context.

- **Look back at the ideas you jotted down when thinking about the question.** Try to link the potential problems you identified with the staging solutions you came up with. Write down clear sentences for each pairing or group. These, after a bit of pruning and sequencing, should form the skeleton of your answer. Begin a new paragraph with each sentence, and use that paragraph to develop and clarify your point. Use quotations from the extract to substantiate your ideas (sometimes you may need two or more paragraphs to explain a complex point well).

- **Conclude your essay.** There are many good ways of ending an essay, but a good fall-back option is to consider audience reaction: how do you want them to react to the extract? In what ways will they be prepared for what follows in the play?

> You are revealing your credentials as a director in two ways here: you are showing your ability to identify problems which are inherent in creating a performance from a specific text and to come up with relevant and imaginative solutions. You should, of course, be prepared to evaluate your solutions.

Blood Wedding

The playwright

Federico García Lorca was born in southern Spain in 1898 to a fairly wealthy family. He had a certain charisma which charmed those in his company and through readings and a growing reputation, he achieved some fame as a poet even before he had any serious collections published. His early poetry books focus on the lives and values of the gypsies of Granada, and on the flamenco they were famous for singing and dancing.

As a young man, Lorca was friendly with both the painter Salvador Dalí and the film maker Luis Buñuel. In the late 1920s, he travelled to the USA where he recorded his impressions of New York City in a long surrealist series of poems (published posthumously as *A Poet in New York* in 1940). Subsequently, he committed himself wholeheartedly to the theatre – though he had always loved the theatre and written plays – and worked with a group of students in a touring company. His major plays were written in the 1930s and include *Blood Wedding* (1932), *Yerma* (1934) and *The House of Bernarda Alba* (1936).

In 1936, shortly after the outbreak of the Spanish Civil War, Lorca was arrested and was shot at a remote farmstead outside Granada. He had made himself unpopular with the rebel right wing not only through his homosexuality but also through his commitment to democracy and popular art. His murder was, and remains, controversial. Laurie Lee describes in *A Rose for Winter*, written in the 1950s, the hush that fell on a room in Andalusia when Lorca's name was mentioned, and the Irish writer Ian Gibson achieved a certain notoriety with his book, *The Assassination of Federico Garcia Lorca* (1983) which examines the circumstances of Lorca's death.

Further reading

For more information about Lorca's life and work, see *Federico García Lorca: A Life* by Ian Gibson (Faber and Faber 1990) and *Lorca: The Theatre Beneath the Sand* by Gwynne Edwards (Marion Boyars 1980).

The play

Blood Wedding is a tragedy. It was inspired by a true story which was reported in the Spanish press: a bride who eloped with her lover before her wedding day from a village near Almería was pursued by villagers; her lover was murdered and she was attacked and left for dead. Although rooted in a real event, the form of the play is tightly and poetically tragic, rather than documentary, with a sense of foreboding established right from the start. A director forming preliminary ideas for a production needs to recognise that the play contains elements of classical tragedy, such as:

➤ An emphasis on the role of fate

➤ The use of verse (especially in the final act)

➤ The use of 'chorus' figures (such as the woodcutters in Act 3 scene 1 and the young girls in Act 3 scene 2 who comment on the action in a ritualised way).

Reed Anderson gives an excellent account of the first performance of Blood Wedding in 1933:

Further reading

Federico García Lorca by Reed Anderson (Palgrave Macmillan 1984).

The critics immediately recognised *Blood Wedding* as a work of innovation for its adventuresome use of an unusually broad range of theatre resources. Also impressive was its consistent high seriousness, and its almost classical delineation of tragic conflict. What people were least prepared for was the mixture of realism and poetic symbolism. Lorca had established the tragic potential of the action during the first two acts in an identifiable social context where social dissonances and contradictions were driving the action towards a tragic crisis.
...

The ... problem of mixing prose and poetry throughout the play had been an over-riding concern of Lorca's in rehearsals, and he tirelessly worked with the cast to maintain a single principle: to make the transitions from prose to poetry as natural as possible by avoiding the declamatory style of acting that was the dominant technique on the stage at the time.

When asked what he would call the most gratifying part of the drama, Lorca said: 'The one where the Moon and Death intervene as elements and symbols of fate. The realism that predominates the tragedy up to that point is broken and disappears to give way to poetic fantasy where I naturally feel as comfortable as a fish in water.'

Characters

The play is structured around the development of the relationships among a small group of characters. Understanding these characters and clarifying their stories – what Stanislavski would call their 'given circumstances' – is key to understanding the play.

One technique which works well in beginning such work is to determine a key moment for each of the characters. For example, the Mother's final speeches in Act 2, as she divides the families into search parties, serve as a key moment for an understanding of her character. On the one hand, she wants her only surviving son to visit on the Felix family the retribution which she thinks is deserved after years of feuding; on the other, she is frightened in the deepest way imaginable that in his desire to wreak violent revenge on Leonardo, her son will himself be killed, leaving her not only defeated, but alone. Her speech dramatises this climax; we can see just how well it articulates the two most important motives in her life.

Choose a character from the play and create a monologue for them, only using lines from the play. You will need to choose lines which you think are crucial to their character, and reassemble them. Omit any lines which serve more to further plot than to evoke character and any which are too firmly tied to a specific situation or listener.

Women

One of the play's main themes concerns the place of women in society. The play begins and ends with women alone on stage. It explores the pressures placed upon women, as mothers, daughters, lovers, wives and widows. Lorca ultimately seems sympathetic to the view that women's lives are constrained by social norms. Indeed, he develops this theme more explicitly in later works: *Yerma* (1934), *Doña Rosita the Spinster* (1935) and in *The House of Bernarda Alba* (1936). When working towards your directorial aims for the play you will need to bear this in mind.

Spain

The critic and writer Raymond Williams recognises the strength of Lorca's work and its place in the European canon. He argues that those who place an 'emphasis on its "Spanish" atmosphere' risk neglecting its more universal messages. Williams agrees, of course, that Lorca drew upon the 'life of the Spanish people' and on their literary heritage and folklore. But he argues that Lorca is first and foremost a European dramatist: 'Lorca's importance is that, drawing strength from a tradition and a people, he found new dramatic forms of contemporary universal experience.'

Further reading

Drama from Ibsen to Brecht by Raymond Williams (Penguin 1973).

Yet this question of 'Spanishness' remains for each new director to confront. Some directors might argue for an Andalusian or flamenco setting, with long, tiered dresses, guitars and so on, on the grounds that the specificity of the setting acts as a doorway to universal truths. Other directors might want to depart from such a setting in order to avoid tourist clichés and worn-out formulas.

Further reading

Do some research into Spain and Andalusia. Some good books to start with are: *South from Granada* by Gerald Brenan (Penguin 2008), *A Rose for Winter* by Laurie Lee (Vintage 2003) and *Lorca's Granada: A Practical Guide* by Ian Gibson (Faber and Faber 1992).

Duende

Students should be guarded when using the term *duende*. Some recent articles and essays use the term very loosely and suggest some degree of misunderstanding. Lorca used the term *duende* in a lecture which he delivered in Buenos Aires in 1933. In Spanish, this word is used to signify 'goblin', and Lorca clearly has the idea of a goblin in mind during this talk, in which he often places the *duende* in opposition to the 'angel'. He tells several stories about what he means by the 'goblin'. One concerns a young flamenco singer, who performs in an Andalusian bar to a predominately gypsy audience. While she performs with accuracy and fluency, expertly and precisely, she gains no applause. One man sarcastically says 'Viva Paris!', by which he means that the performance has the sophistication of the big city but lacks the soul the gypsies expect from their flamenco tradition. The singer, stung by this, downs a drink of *aguardiente* ('firewater') and sings again, this time attending neither to accuracy nor to 'voice, breath or colour'. She replaces the 'angel' of technical expertise with the 'goblin' of suffering and truth.

Further reading

The whole of Lorca's lecture, translated into English by Christopher Maurer, appears in *Deep Song and Other Prose* by Federico García Lorca, edited by Christopher Maurer (Marion Boyars 1983).

So, Lorca uses *duende* to mean the prioritising of the emotional truth of a performance over its technical mastery. He claims that it is in music, dance and spoken poetry that the 'goblin' is most likely to be found. He sees the writer, composer and dance teacher working with the performer to allow the goblin to appear. The goblin is most likely to appear when 'a living body' interprets material.

We are all familiar with this conception of *duende*. Some of us may have grimaced at classically trained violinists turning their hands to an Irish reel: while the notes are all there and the intonation is perfect, something crucial is missing. In Lorca's terms: too much 'angel', too little 'goblin'.

So, while we cannot say that there is *duende* in *Blood Wedding* itself, we can say that – to use Lorca's terminology – the play provides ample material whereby a gifted and inspired performer can allow the 'goblin' to appear.

Directorial aims

When you've read the play and undertaken the work on the text we've suggested here, listened to some flamenco music (to access *duende*!) and read about Lorca's life, then you will be ready to construct directorial aims for your imagined production of the play.

> To help construct your directorial aims, choose a quotation from the play which you feel succinctly encapsulates a particular aspect you'd like to bring out in your production. Drawing up a shortlist of such quotations will give you a good insight into the key themes and emotions of the play.

One of the beauties of *Blood Wedding*, which the critic Reed Anderson alludes to, is the way in which each act, though unequivocally part of a whole, treats the same material in a slightly different way, just as three movements in a musical composition might. Act 1, in such a scheme, is the most realistic and naturalistic of them all.

Act 1

During the 19th century, there was a great emphasis placed on **realism** in drama. Many theatre companies spent enormous amounts of time and money creating the realistic appearance of the play's setting. Writers used contemporary and recognisable situations, and dialogue moved towards a more natural form of speech. In serious theatres, a significant change in acting style emerged, realised most fully in the work of the Russian director Stanislavski. He recognised that realism worked through metonymy, and he devised a series of approaches to the text which allowed actors to explore this device, so as to create psychologically realistic characters. Many terms from Stanislavski's writing have entered into general use in the theatre.

We must be careful not to confuse realism with **naturalism**. Naturalism was a philosophical approach to life which was derived from Charles Darwin's work. Naturalist writers, such as Émile Zola in France, Henrik Ibsen in Norway and Thomas Hardy in England, followed Darwin's view that people (or species) are shaped by a combination of heredity and environment. Their writings place great emphasis on the significance of parentage and location to character.

> Naturalist playwrights often incorporate realism. Lorca is unusual, however, in that he moves towards a more poetic, *unrealistic* form of drama in which naturalist ideas are worked through.

Naturalist plays usually present a tense situation which is strained to breaking point by a small external intervention. They typically set up the situation, followed by the intervention, the ensuing tension, the breaking point and the aftermath. In this first act, then, Lorca establishes the situation and the tension, in a naturalist manner. We see the characters interacting with one another in the three households. We know that the planned wedding will provide the 'breaking point' to occur in Act 2, leaving us with Act 3 in which we will be shown the aftermath.

> The nature of the writing in Act 1 encourages a director to approach the play in a Stanislavskian style, identifying subtext, motivation, objectives and so on.

Even in Act 1, Lorca moves his audience very gently towards the poetry of Act 3 without disrupting the largely realistic world he has established. In scene 2, we hear Leonardo's wife and her mother

> **Further reading**
>
> Lorca gave a lecture 'On Lullabies' in Madrid in 1928. You can find it in *Deep Song and Other Prose* by Federico García Lorca, edited by Christopher Maurer (Marion Boyars 1983).

singing a lullaby. While Lorca builds this verse on a traditional Spanish model, his choice of imagery reflects the particular themes and imagery of the play.

Act 2

Further viewing

Watch Carlos Saura's flamenco ballet adaptation of *Blood Wedding* (1981). He shows how the simple tragic tale is closely aligned with the spirit of flamenco: its pain, passions and withheld eroticism. Curiously, perhaps, Saura declines to present Act 3. There are also no woodcutters (scene 1 is reduced to a stylised knife fight) and no mourning (scene 2 is reduced to one despairing gesture from the Bride).

The audience at the first performance of *Blood Wedding* was impressed by the way in which Lorca combined increasing tension among his characters with a spectacle of dance and music. In many places in Act 2, his writing has a cinematic quality, alternating intimate conversations with large, group actions. This poses something of a problem for a stage director: the intimate conversations must remain just that, while the dances and wedding festivities should continue unchecked as a constant backdrop to the action. You will need to develop a clear idea about how you're going to manage this.

The problem facing the director of *Blood Wedding* in Act 3 is the almost complete transition which is made to poetry. There is poetry both in the stage imagery – the woodcutters' appearance, the moon, the violins and so on – and in the language. The best advice for a director here is that which the director Peter Brook has given in other contexts: *trust the text*. As soon as a director loses their nerve, the audience will spot the compromises which have been made and will not be drawn into the play. One tentative line from the actor playing the moon risks everything. One of the most important things that a director can do when rehearsing Act 3 is to impress upon the cast the importance of every single word and action.

The use of poetry and symbolism in *Blood Wedding* helps to make the characters universal as well as individual, which is supported by the lack of proper character names.

Design

A director might go through Lorca's set instructions with a designer. There is an important, symbolic use of colour in them, and each scene appears to have its own colour scheme. When thinking about design you might also like to think about Lorca's own drawings.

Further reading

See *Lorca: The Drawings, Their Relation to the Poet's Life and Work* by Helen Oppenheimer (Franklin Watts 1987).

The Good Person of Szechwan

The playwright

Bertolt Brecht was both a playwright and a director of his own and others' plays. Although a director should not feel at all obliged to follow Brecht's models when devising a production of *The Good Person of Szechwan*, it is necessary to be aware of the ways in which Brecht imagined plays such as his should be performed.

It is possible that you will have already studied Brecht at AS and will therefore be familiar with his work. However, it is still necessary to remind yourself of the principles of his practice before beginning work on this play.

Theatre for Brecht was a place where social and moral instruction and improvement should take place. He wanted his spectators, after they had watched a play, to go out and change the world – to put right the wrongs in society that they had witnessed on stage.

Further reading

For further information on Brecht see *Bertolt Brecht: Chaos, According to Plan* by John Fuegi (Cambridge University Press 1987), *Brecht Sourcebook*, edited by Henry Bial and Carol Martin (Routledge 1999) and *The Theatre of Bertolt Brecht* by John Willett (Methuen 1977).

The play

The play is told in a deliberately naïve style. It doesn't contain any complex poetry or difficult imagery and the narrative progresses quickly. While some characters are given complex roles, others have simple, one-dimensional parts. The language is simple and direct, characterised by a finely judged rhythm which is almost rhetorical. Relatively long speeches are easy to deliver in an entertaining style because they are written in this idiom (which John Willett expertly recreates in his translation of the play).

A parable

Brecht calls the play a 'parable', which is a richly evocative term. It has religious connotations, of course, but more importantly it also has didactic overtones: Brecht is trying to teach the audience something. As with so many parables, the question of *what* is being taught is somewhat ambiguous. An audience may be unsure whether to side with Shen Te or Shui Ta, and a good director should ensure that this ambivalence is maintained. In the end, we must sympathise to some extent with both characters.

Casting

In their introduction to the play, Willett and Ralph Manheim place great store on the casting of Shen Te. They make a number of key points. Firstly, they draw attention to the 'neuter' title of the play in the original German. Their translation of the title uses what in English is a rather clumsy phrase: 'the good person'. Earlier translations used 'the good woman'. They argue, persuasively, not only that they are accurately translating the original German, but that by giving the play this title they are maintaining the ambiguity of its values.

Further reading

The Good Person of Szechwan by Bertolt Brecht, translated by John Willett (Methuen 1985).

They counsel against casting for the cliché of the 'lovable hooker'. Presenting Shen Te in this way prompts a hackneyed understanding from the audience and fails to maintain a balance between her generosity of spirit and Shui Ta's selfishness. To this end, they even advise directors to consider casting a man in the part.

Brecht's theatre

Brecht was heavily influenced by Chinese theatre of the period and the work of the actor Mei Langfang in particular. Chinese theatre made use of symbols, which an audience recognised quickly in performance, allowing for a pared-down style both in design and acting. Recognised gestures were used to represent the opening of a door, so that no actual door was needed on stage. The stage was always the same, though different items of furniture were brought on and off to represent various locations. The actors ignored the fourth wall and positioned themselves in a deliberate way to be seen as clearly as possible. To demonstrate that they saw their performance as alien to themselves, they would look at their own actions and comment upon them through gestures to the audience. This ensured that the audience thought seriously about the actions of the play rather than empathising with the characters. Brecht recognised that in this way the Chinese actor was demonstrating or 'quoting' the character rather than *becoming* the character, and he realised how important this was in enabling the audience to think about the social messages behind the performance.

Chinese theatre

> For instance, a general in Chinese theatre would wear a number of ribbons on his shoulder to represent his status in the army, while differently coloured patches sewn onto silk robes indicated poverty.

Today, the theatre most closely associated with Brecht is epic theatre. Epic theatre is an umbrella term that encompasses

Epic theatre

different techniques and aspects of performance. However, it is characterised by two important rules:

> The message conveyed by the play must be clear at all times

> The audience (or 'spectators') must retain a critical awareness that allows them to focus and reflect upon the message.

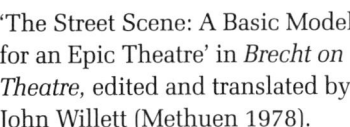

Further reading

'The Street Scene: A Basic Model for an Epic Theatre' in *Brecht on Theatre*, edited and translated by John Willett (Methuen 1978).

Brecht wanted epic acting to surprise the spectators and to encourage them to question why characters acted in such a manner. This was to be achieved by removing the familiar. In his essay 'The Street Scene: A Basic Model for an Epic Theatre' Brecht writes about 'acting in quotation marks': actors should present a character in the same way that a witness to an accident might present their information to a court. There should be a distance between the actor and the events that their character is experiencing.

The German word for this dramatic device is *Verfremdungseffekt*. This is often translated as 'alienation effect', however it is perhaps clearer when translated as 'making strange'.

This contrasts to realist theatre, in which the audience are not acknowledged by the actors and an imaginary fourth wall is established. In Brecht's system the audience *are* a recognised part of the experience. The actors often address the audience directly, breaking the fourth wall, in order to explain their actions. Hearing all three sides of an argument, removed from the actual event, allows the audience to listen dispassionately and pass critical judgement. When a scene is played for a second time, both the actors and the audience can be more objective.

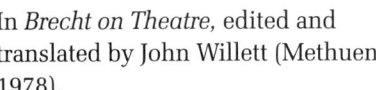

Further reading

In *Brecht on Theatre*, edited and translated by John Willett (Methuen 1978).

Brecht detailed the differences between dramatic theatre and epic theatre in an essay entitled 'Theatre for Pleasure or Theatre for Instruction':

> The dramatic theatre's spectator says: Yes, I have felt like that too – Just like me – It's only natural – It'll never change – The sufferings of this man appal me, because they are inescapable – That's great art; it all seems the most obvious thing in the world – I weep when they weep, I laugh when they laugh.
>
> The epic theatre's spectator says: I'd never have thought it – That's not the way – That's extraordinary, hardly believable – It's got to stop – The sufferings of this man appal me, because they are unnecessary – That's great art: nothing obvious in it – I laugh when they weep, I weep when they laugh.

Didactic means intended to instruct. Dialectic refers to the testing of truth through discussion – in simple terms, a debate. For a play to be truly dialectic, both sides of the argument needed to be given equal presentation.

Brecht wanted his theatre to be both **didactic** and **dialectic**. Through his work he wanted spectators to learn about the world in which they lived, to understand how the political and social world worked, and to see that they could make a difference to it. He was particularly keen that his plays were seen by the working classes, who did not often go to the theatre.

Gestus

The style of acting required by Brecht is referred to as gestic acting. Actors demonstrated social attitudes in such a way that they could be understood by those who were deaf: that is to say, no words were needed to communicate the social positions of the characters in relation to one another.

The **gestus** is a freeze-frame moment that an actor uses to sum up the social position of their character. Everything an audience needs to know about the character's social status in relation to the message of the play should be clear from this moment. Sometimes the moment is marked by a literal freeze-frame, for instance on the entrance of the character.

Sets

Brechtian sets were intended to be representative of a place, rather than suggesting to the audience that they had actually been transported to the location of the play. Thus a room might be represented by a piece of furniture, with no walls and doors on stage.

It's important to note, however, that Brecht did not advocate minimalism, as is commonly thought. Many of the sets for his plays were complicated structures, involving scaffolding, rostra and towers. The actors would often construct the set during the play: items were brought on and off in order to change the basic outline or shape of the stage. The overall effect was still merely to *suggest* a location, and the sets were constructed to look as if they might only survive the duration of the performance.

The mechanics of theatre were in view at all times, so that an audience could never forget that they were watching a play. Thus, lights remained visible, and any movement of scenery was done in full light in front of the audience, rather than hidden behind a curtain or blackout. The actors remained on stage when not in character to observe the performance. Costume rails were also visible and an actor changed character in view of the audience, so that they could not make the mistake of equating the actor with the character.

Props

Although Brecht was against scenic realism, he did prefer the props that were used to be the real thing. This was partly because he felt that the use of a representative item for a prop would confuse an audience, who would be wondering why an actor was using (in an extreme example) a banana to write with, when a pen would be more suitable. In addition, Brecht liked actors to use items that had a sense of history and social significance. So, if a character was the prime minister, for example, he might use a pen that had actually been used by a prime minister to sign an important treaty, rather than just any old pen. The actor would have some reverence for the prop, which would affect his use of it, which would in turn help to inform the audience about the importance of that moment in the play.

> Brecht also liked props that had been hand-crafted. Even a wooden bowl used by a peasant should be made by a craftsman, so that the actor would have an appreciation of the effort involved in making the bowl, which would impact upon their performance.

Brecht also used full and half-masks in a number of his productions. This allowed him to contrast masked characters with those who didn't have a mask.

Augusto Boal

The Good Person of Szechwan invites its spectators to discuss whether 'goodness' is valid or even possible in a flawed society. The characters of Shen Te and Shui Ta dramatically represent this dialectic. You might like to consider a production in which the audience are invited to contribute their own opinions to a discussion, mediated by a kind of 'master of ceremonies'. This is the kind of theatre advocated by Augusto Boal, for whom theatre does not provide passive entertainment but is a forum for debate, education and revolution.

Background

Boal is an innovative director and political activist who was born in 1931 in Rio de Janeiro, Brazil. He is the founder of the Theatre of the Oppressed and it is for his work with this socio-political theatre that he has attained international stature as a theatre practitioner. Boal's ideas are politically provocative; in the 1960s he was branded a cultural activist and was considered a threat by the military in Brazil who ran the country undemocratically. As a consequence, he was arrested in 1971, tortured and exiled to Argentina, where he published his first book *Theatre of the Oppressed* in 1973. Following the end of Brazil's military junta, Boal returned to Rio de Janeiro in 1986, where he still lives.

In some ways, Boal's work is a direct descendant of Brecht's, in that the audience are expected to take an active part in performances, even calling out and expressing indignation at a character's behaviour. For Boal, a production which discourages such involvement is 'closed' theatre and denies the audience a natural channel for their feelings and responses. Boal advocates widespread use of 'open' theatres which place less emphasis on performance and more on participation. His technique places great emphasis on working with people on rehearsal techniques without a performance in sight. The techniques themselves thus become games whose function is not entirely 'theatrical'. Boal subverts – or reclaims, depending on your point of view – the bourgeois values of theatre.

Forum Theatre

Forum Theatre was devised as a result of work Boal did in Peru in 1973 as part of a scheme to address illiteracy in village communities. Boal calls Forum Theatre a 'collective rehearsal for reality'. A scene is presented to the audience in which the protagonist is confronted by a problem which they fail to overcome. The audience members, or as Boal prefers to call them, the 'spect-actors', are invited to replace the protagonist and re-enact, more successfully perhaps, the situation. The actors improvise their responses to the volunteer's new course of action; this allows all the spectators to explore alternative modes of behaviour and move towards the empowerment of hitherto marginalised members of society.

> In Boal's work, this problem is usually a socio-political problem related to undemocratic oppression; however, the method can be used in relation to a wide range of problems.

> Sometimes this intervention by the audience is managed by a Joker character (the figure from a pack of cards) who manages the situation and moves from one protagonist to the next as the problem is explored.

Could this kind of intervention between performers and audience members be used effectively in an unconventional production of *The Good Person of Szechwan*?

Directorial aims

The play is written in a consistent style and nearly every page places important clues before us as to performance and acting style. Scene 3 includes many characteristic elements of Brecht's approach. The opening is typical in its use of simple symbolism (the tattered clothes and the rope), humour and in its presentation of characters who are arguably more important in terms of *what* they represent than for who they are.

While the opening stage directions help to explain the situation for director and cast, they do not provide a method for realising the scene. The aeroplane could be audible rather than visible; the willow tree might be entirely imagined or it could just be a section of all-purpose scaffolding. The director needs to clarify these elements in the context of clear, over-arching directorial aims.

The prostitutes, Sun and Shen Te, play clichéd parts, and their lines at the start are deliberately hackneyed. The energetic dialogue between them develops the story quickly; this is then interrupted by a considerable change of pace in Sun's long speech. Sun's innocent inclusion in his account of so many words from the lexical field of 1940s flying makes it a masterpiece of comic writing which belies the personal despair it articulates. Shen Te's reaction and the story she tells of the crane reveal her empathy but also her distance from Sun's truth: she turns his reality into a parable of her own.

A director following Boal's example might interrupt the scene at this moment and invite the audience to comment on the action – perhaps even decide whether Sun should hang himself or not. In a way, Brecht does something similar to Boal's dramatic techniques in the text itself. She Te speaks directly to the audience, breaking down the 'fourth wall' and sympathising with Sun's lot: 'Only a little is needed/ Before men start throwing/ Their unbearable life away.' Indeed, Brecht seems to signal an important change in Sun's demeanour after this speech, when he asks Shen Te, 'Tell me about yourself.'

When staging *The Good Person of Szechwan*, a director needs to balance the rather stylised characterisation, and the energetic and often comic storytelling with the serious social and political issues with which Brecht aims to provoke the audience.

> **Scene 3**
>
> Sun's speech is characterised by the same humour which brings a sense of 'serious fun' to so much of Brecht's writing.
>
> If you chose such a staging of this scene, you would of course need to be able to justify your decision very clearly and with a demonstrable understanding of Boal's work.

A View from the Bridge

The playwright

Arthur Miller (1915–2005) was an American playwright whose status in American letters grew prominently during the second half of the 20th century and remains very high today. Miller's most celebrated works are *All My Sons* (1947), *Death of a Salesman* (1949), *The Crucible* (1953) and *A View from the Bridge* (1955). His plays often reflect, in different ways, the political controversies of the period in which they were written.

In 1956, Miller married the actress Marilyn Monroe, although their marriage ended in 1961. In 2002, Miller was awarded Spain's Principe de Asturias Prize for Literature as an 'undisputed master of modern drama'. He died on 10 February 2005.

The play

A View from the Bridge juxtaposes stylised classicism with realistic naturalism. Miller achieves an elegant harmony between its theme – Italian immigrants living in New York – and its style – it is a classical play for the 20th century. Actors and directors must work to convey this harmony to an audience when developing a production of the play.

A View from the Bridge has an interesting history. Miller first wrote it as a verse play, but after this was unsuccessful in performance, he rewrote it in prose, adding new material, especially to the female parts, and dividing it into two acts. Rewriting it in this way softened the impact of the classical model and emphasised the realistic elements of the play.

Realistic and non-realistic features

Draw up a list of realistic and non-realistic features in the play. Imagine you are preparing, as a director, a production. The following table sketches out some key ideas to get you started. There may be more features which you might want to add to the list. You will want to explore each idea in greater depth and with more precise reference to the text.

Realistic features	Non-realistic features
Language	The use of a narrator/chorus figure
Themes (such as family, immigration, the individual in the 'land of the free', sex and gender)	The set (as described in the text)
Content and detail	The Sicilians' knowledge of English
Costume	Symbolism (such as Rodolfo's idea of a motorcycle)

Practical exercise

In groups, having amended the lists of features to your satisfaction, allocate one feature to each student (in small groups, each student might have more than one feature to look at). Write at least one paragraph on your allocated feature, exploring its meaning and finding precise moments in the text which exemplify it. Present your conclusions to one another.

What conclusions can you draw from this set of oppositions?

A director must make decisions about whether to emphasise the realistic or non-realistic features of the play. It would be surprising, for instance, if a director who had opted for a realistic set should ask his actors to deliver the lines in an over-stylised and rhythmic style more appropriate to a verse play.

However, there is a danger of over-emphasising one set of features at the expense of the other. A director who prioritises the **realism** of the play risks undermining its classical weight and significance.

The role of Alfieri may become muddled and peripheral, and the huge weight of Eddie's suppressed fears and desires may be lightened and rendered less significant. However, a director who emphasises the **classical** features may fall into the same trap which Miller fell into with his original verse drama: losing the sympathy and interest of a modern audience, and making the whole thing feel too artificial.

Miller's description of a set at the beginning of the text reveals this essential ambiguity by mixing a stylised view of a tenement block with ramps representing the street, with a more realistic depiction of Eddie's living room. A director needs to come up with a creative way of keeping alive both the classical and contemporary elements of the play.

Classical drama has always exerted an influence to some degree or other on western literary drama. Here is a list of some of the key themes which it deals with:

- Illicit passion/sexual taboo/incest versus honourable love/lawful marriage
- The conflict between reason and desire
- The tension between good and evil
- Gender stereotyping (women passive/men active)
- The role of fate
- The structure of political hierarchies and power struggles
- The relationship between physical and moral sickness
- The concept of heroism
- The mythical heritage of the protagonists
- The intervention of the gods

To what extend do these 'classical' themes emerge in *A View from the Bridge*?

Eddie is clearly the hero. He is powerful – in that he can offer accommodation to Beatrice's cousins – but he is also flawed. In exploring the consequences of his flaws, Miller is following the classical model. As Beatrice is aware, Eddie has suppressed sexual desire for Catherine, his niece, and many of his comments to her disguise his own discomfort at this. He does not want her to look like a film star because he cannot cope with the feelings that such an appearance might arouse in him. Similarly, his comments about Rodolfo, which imply that Rodolfo is gay, suggest that Eddie is uncomfortable with the idea of homosexuality, and that he may feel some attraction himself for the young man: 'It's wonderful. He sings, he cooks, he could make dresses …'

Classical drama

Think about…

How could you design the play – including the set, costume and wigs – in a way which blends both the classical and the contemporary?

Further study

Aristotle's *Poetics* gives an early critique of the nature of tragedy; look at it to find a precise analysis of the genre.

Characters

Think about…

A classical tragedy should invite an audience to sympathise with the main protagonist, not just condemn them. What elements of Eddie's character help us to sympathise with him? Even when he is kissing the two young lovers (kisses which mingle lust and aggression) our shock should not cancel out *all* our sympathy for him.

Miller brilliantly provides a key moment which dramatises these suppressed emotions: when Eddie kisses first Catherine and then Rodolfo he makes his feelings for the young people explicit in a way which ideally should shock a contemporary audience as much as it would have done an American audience in the 1950s.

The kiss itself is a key moment in the balance between the classical and the contemporary. Its shock is contemporary and the reaction of those on stage should be so, too, but the idea of an action such as this – one which is not everyday or intrinsically 'realistic' – is essentially classical.

Another symbolic moment occurs when Eddie challenges Rodolfo by offering to teach him boxing. This action is complex and deserves detailed attention. Eddie has been stung into action by the romantic behaviour of the youngsters who are dancing to the music on the record player. The dancing is presented as a 'feminine' activity; Eddie mistrusts Rodolfo and his complex emotions towards the two are clouding his judgement. By challenging Rodolfo to fight, he is suppressing his own more feminine side and accentuating the macho, masculine world of Sicilian men. Eddie is behaving like an animal threatened by a stronger male in the pack: he is trying to humiliate Rodolfo and, in dramatic terms, is foreshadowing the climax of the play.

In classical tragedy, the protagonist was conventionally a noble or a king. Miller appears to be eschewing this tradition: a longshoreman is hardly a nobleman. He undermines the sense of a structured social hierarchy which the classical model promotes, by saying that the life of a longshoreman is just as significant – both to the individual and to society – as that of a king or a noble. However, it should be noted that Eddie is indeed 'noble' in his own world. As a member of the Italian immigrant community, he has a certain standing. Without such a standing, his behaviour at the end of the play would be diminished in its effect. Miller therefore subverts the classical requirement that a protagonist is of noble birth while simultaneously reinforcing it.

Modern 'gods'

In the ancient Greek world, gods were used to explain the apparently irrational behaviour of men and women. So, who are the 'gods' of 1950s America to whom people's behaviour was attributed?

Because of the influence of cinema, most new plays in the 1950s were realistic dramas, played by and large on realistic sets. Hand in hand with realism – but by no means the same thing – is the concept of naturalism. In the play, the comfortable domestic setting of Eddie's household is disrupted by Catherine's growing independence; however, her independence is shaped and confined by Eddie's expectations for her, by the class and culture into which she has been born and by the work she has done at school and college. The 'gods' of her heredity and environment have foretold her future.

Practical exercise

Each character in the play has a back story: what Stanislavski would call their 'given circumstances'. It's amazing how much detail and information Miller packs into the play without it appearing contrived. Try composing a monologue for each character in which they relate their back story in their own voice. You'll find plenty of lines already in the play, waiting to be assembled.

Think about...

Miller married Marilyn Monroe in 1956, the same year in which he revised *A View from the Bridge* (he wrote the original verse drama the year before, in 1955): can you imagine Monroe playing the part of Catherine? Visualising Monroe in this role – or at least a younger wannabe Monroe – might help us sympathise a little more with Eddie's behaviour.

See page 63 for more on naturalism.

The second 'god' of 1950s New York was **Sigmund Freud**. The aspect of Freud's psychoanalytical work which most concerns us here is the idea of suppressed or subconscious desires and urges. It is clear both to the audience and to Beatrice that Eddie's head has been turned by Catherine and her youthful glamour. When, finally, Beatrice confronts the audience with the idea that Eddie is subconsciously attracted to Catherine, the open reference to incest is shocking. Yet Eddie is not portrayed as straightforwardly 'guilty'; Beatrice seems to understand that while this is something Eddie must overcome, he has not instigated it and that he is a victim of his subconscious urges.

Eddie's repeated insinuations about Rodolfo suggest that he suspects he is homosexual. In the social climate of the time, this was perhaps characteristic behaviour for men like Eddie who adopted a macho approach to life. However, a more Freudian explanation of Eddie's behaviour might be that he feels homosexual urges himself, thus intensifying his jealousy of Catherine and his own insecurity. Once again, Eddie is a victim of urges which he tries to suppress, but cannot entirely control.

So, naturalism and Freudian psychoanalysis, Miller seems to suggest, are the modern 'gods' determining our fate. By foreshadowing key events – for instance in the boxing scene, where the final fight is prefigured – Miller is also able to integrate Greek ideas of prophecy and fate into a 20th-century play.

Directorial aims

We've seen that the episode which climaxes with Eddie's kisses and the one in which Eddie challenges Rodolfo to box are both important. Beginning your rehearsals of the play with an analysis of these two scenes will help to establish key moods and methods. For instance, we can understand what drives Eddie and how those around him react to his behaviour. After Eddie kisses Rodolfo, Catherine stares at him 'in horror. Rodolfo is rigid. They are like animals that have torn at one another and broken up without a decision, each waiting for the other's mood'. At this moment, the tensions underlying the relationships in the play emerge into the light. Exploring the tensions at this point will help to bring hints of them to the fore when rehearsing earlier episodes.

Think about...

Although the play is not formally divided into scenes, it does contain discrete episodes. Focusing on what you think are the most important episodes can be an excellent way of establishing the underlying themes and dramatic issues in the play.

Opening scene

The opening scene asks director and actor to clarify their views on the whole play. Without a clear understanding of the dramatic role of Alfieri and the opening monologue, no production of the play is going to be successful. The speech itself manifests the juxtaposition of the classical and the contemporary. The language, though heightened and beautifully rhythmic, is the language of New York – 'My wife has warned me, so have my friends; they tell me the people in this neighbourhood lack elegance, glamour. After all, who have I dealt with in my life?' – but the dramatic function is that of the Greek chorus. Alfieri stands outside the action – he introduces Eddie to us here – but he is also part of it. Getting the tone and pace of this opening right and establishing the 'New York' and 'classical' elements of the play here is crucial.

When he rewrote the play, as we have seen, Miller divided his material into two acts. Act 1 looks forward, with some dread, to the future of the illegal immigrants and Eddie's family; in Act 2 that future arrives. It might be helpful for a director to clarify the questions that are left unresolved at the end of Act 1. In a small group, list the key issues and establish accurately how they have been left. There's usually an interval between the acts. What would an engaged audience talk about? Spend time yourselves discussing Act 1 before moving on.

Language and style

The language in the play can be an issue for actors: at least, for those actors who don't come from New York! Miller catches the rhythms of a New York dialect with an honest accuracy, and finding these rhythms is essential work for an actor preparing one of these roles. Sometimes Miller suggests accent through spelling, sometimes through distinctive syntax: 'Well he ain't exackly funny, but he's always like makin' remarks like, you know? He comes around.'

The Sicilian arrivals are mysteriously able to speak clear English, yet they still adopt an Italianate syntax: 'We stand around all day in the piazza listening to the fountain like birds. Everyone waits only for the train.'

Think about...

Miller's first version of *A View from the Bridge* was a verse play (see page 73). Exploring the similarities the existing play has to a verse play can be fruitful. Identify the natural rhythms of the language: although the play is no longer in verse, it still requires considered delivery.

Social context

Arthur Miller lived and worked through the anti-communist hysteria of the 1950s. Men in prominent jobs were asked, often threateningly, to name those they suspected of communist sympathies or ties. Some of Miller's friends cooperated with this activity, but Miller himself refused. Though later acquitted on appeal, in 1957 Miller was found guilty of contempt of Congress for refusing to reveal the names of members of a literary group who were suspected of Communist leanings. Both *The Crucible* and *A View from the Bridge* confront the theme of betrayal which, as we now understand, was something Miller had experienced himself; while he refused to betray friends and associates, many others did not.

The 1950s was also a period of rapid social change and economic migration. Rodolfo and Marco are peasants who have illegally escaped from a land where there is little work and thus are surviving by breaking the law. It is no surprise that they have difficulty squaring this with the image of America as the land of the free. Eddie is also still a peasant and a survivor; his work is not guaranteed and he adopts a lax approach to honesty.

Further reading

John Berger writes in the introduction to his trilogy *Into Their Labours* (Penguin 1992) that in western Europe, if economic planners have their way, there will be 'no more peasants within 25 years'. He regards peasants as 'survivors' who live from hand to mouth, and is appalled by the way in which society taxes them, creating a sometimes insuperable burden which they must carry.

In light of this, think about the significance of the play's title. Of course, it immediately conjures up the Brooklyn Bridge, a famous landmark in New York. We might also think about how the wealthy of America travel over the bridge in cars while the poor live down below, on the shoreline among the docks and dockers. We might perhaps think about the way in which homeless people gather beneath bridges for shelter, often in discomfort and cold. If this is the 'view' from such a bridge then, as comfy theatregoers, looking down at the hardships of the urban peasant might be uncomfortable.

> **Practical exercise**
>
> Discuss in your group how the play portrays the 'death of the peasant'. What other contemporary political resonances does the play have?

The Trial

Introduction to the play

The Trial (1971) is an adaptation of the novel of the same name by Franz Kafka (published in 1925). Kafka's novel is fairly long, and while Steven Berkoff's adaptation uses key images, motifs and dialogue from it, it does not attempt to give a page-by-page account of the original book. Indeed, Berkoff omits the end of the story as it is given in Kafka's novel.

Kafka was a Czech who wrote in German. He published little during his lifetime and asked his friend Max Brod to burn all his papers and unpublished work after his death. Brod did not do so, however, and instead oversaw their publication.

The playwright

> **Further reading**
>
> Brod's decision to publish Kafka's papers was not an uncontroversial one, as Milan Kundera's book *Testaments Betrayed*, translated by Linda Asher (Faber and Faber 2004), makes clear.

Kafka's novel *The Trial* is a modernist text in that it prioritises **metaphor** over **metonymy**. The nightmare world it creates, of blundering, cold bureaucracy, combines a surreal sense of imagery with genuine terror and nihilism. Its metaphorical writing requires readers to contribute actively to an interpretation of the text. Kafka provides some enigmatic clues in the naming of his characters: the man undergoing the trial is called 'K.' and the man who arrests him is called 'Franz'. The arrest which K. experiences is ambiguous: on some levels he seems to be able to continue leading a 'normal' life, however he suffers on a psychological level from the knowledge that he is a prisoner of a pointless, inescapable system.

> For a discussion of the difference between metaphor and metonymy see page 49.

Berkoff dramatises not so much the narrative development of Kafka's novel but its *content*: he explores the emotions which the novel creates and its imagery. The subjectivity of his treatment coincides with the subjective nature of Kafka's view of the world.

A reading of Kafka's novel can give us an insight into Berkoff's play – for instance, much of Kafka's The Trial contains comic elements which might make a director look more readily for opportunities for laughter in Berkoff's text. However, a director of *The Trial* needs to recognise that, ultimately, our priority is to understand Berkoff's reading rather than Kafka's original novel.

> A simple reading of the novel is that it is an analogy for a nihilist sense of being: the angst felt due to an existence which seems blighted by suffering and pointlessness. Just because this reading is simple does not mean it is wrong!

The playwright

Performance style

> If you studied Berkoff as a practitioner in your AS course, this will prove a great advantage. However, you will need to use your theoretical knowledge of Berkoff to inform your *own* directorial and performance decisions.

Although the themes of *The Trial* echo the concerns and politics of the early 1970s when it was devised and first produced, it was also conceived as a vehicle for Berkoff's style of bravura performance. A production of the play should be aware of Berkoff's original performance, while undertaking a new interpretation of the text.

Berkoff's style as a theatrical performer in the 1970s relied chiefly on the actor's use of the body. Sets were basic and mime was fundamental. Gestures, especially facial expressions, were routinely exaggerated, often grotesquely and purely for effect.

Metamorphosis

In 1969, Berkoff adapted Kafka's short story *Metamorphosis* in a way which relied heavily upon the physical approach of the company and Berkoff himself especially. The story centres on the absurdist notion that a young man turns overnight into a gigantic insect. Berkoff insisted that this metamorphosis should be portrayed not through costume or special effects, but simply through the use of his body: 'I played it as a human being locked within the carapace of the beetle, and I physically attempted to enact the rhythms of an insect and its frenetic scurrying movements. The use of mime made this possible.'

Further reading

Steven Berkoff and the Theatre of Self-Performance by Robert Cross (Manchester University Press 2004).

The set, following French models of total theatre espoused by Antonin Artaud and Jean-Louis Barrault, was simple but symbolic: 'A skeletal framework of a giant insect is stretched across the stage – this serves as the home of the family or as the carapace. The stage is void of all props – everything is mimed – apart from three black stools (metal) situated equidistant downstage for the family to use.'

Further reading

For more information about Berkoff see *Steven Berkoff and the Theatre of Self-Performance* by Robert Cross (Manchester University Press 2004) and *The Theatre of Steven Berkoff* (a collection of performance photographs) by Steven Berkoff (Methuen 1992).

Photographs of the production show the kind of physical demands it made upon the actors; at one point Berkoff hung from the scaffolding by only his ankles. In a 1986 revival, with the Samsa/insect character played by Tim Roth, photos show how the actor, dressed in the kind of smart wear Kafka might have been comfortable in, clung to the floor as a fly clings to a ceiling, adapting every gesture to this surreal role.

Berkoff's performance style can be summed up as being characterised by the following:

➢ Exaggerated, physical theatre

➢ Exaggerated gestures and contorted body shapes

➢ Grotesque movements and facial expressions

➢ A tendency towards simple, monochrome sets and costumes

➢ A refusal to shy away from difficult staging

➢ A confrontational manner.

The play

In many ways, the script of *The Trial* represents a record of a production, and thus some of its stage directions lack the clarity we would normally expect from a play script. For example, the first set of stage directions includes complex instructions, such as 'A piano begins a gentle melody which fades with a crashing Bach'. This instruction combines a certain precision with a perplexing vagueness. A director has to select the key elements (here, they seem to be the aural impact of a 'gentle' melody which ends with 'crashing') and make them their own.

Similarly, we are told that the cast 'enter one by one – on the stage 10 screens are placed – standing upright'. The size and nature of these screens are not specified, leaving them open to wide interpretation. In many productions, frames about the size of door frames are used, which the actors move and manipulate (as Berkoff specifies) to create various sets.

Each production of *The Trial* must find a new language with which to stage Berkoff's text. Directors should work with their casts to rehearse and improvise sequences of physical theatre and mime, and the individual strengths and skills of actors need to be employed to create an atmosphere of muscular tension on stage.

In preparing for the examination, you will need to have a considered style in mind for the play, which you are able to articulate cogently and clearly. To have developed this, you will need to have worked as a director on several extracts of the play – if not the whole text – leading rehearsals and experimenting with the performance strengths of a cast. Throughout rehearsals you should note down your experimental process – trying things which do not work can be just as illuminating as discovering a successful technique. You will also need to be able to analyse your successful final work in order to share an understanding of why certain approaches work in performance for an audience.

When beginning work on the text, focus initially on the stage directions before moving on to the spoken text. Work through the whole play and collect all the stage directions, then rehearse them together; this will provide an extraordinary insight into Berkoff's dramatic method (for instance: 'Street noises. Traffic sounds. They mime taxi ride. They speak without communicating to each other.')

Antonin Artaud (1896–1948) represents the other end of the performance spectrum from Stanislavski. He did not want to represent reality in his productions – he wanted to transcend it. He did not want his actors to be limited by the representation of real people with real psychologies, but wanted them to access completely new areas of experience, divorced from the everyday

Style

Further reading

You can find the script of *The Trial* in *Three Theatre Adaptations from Franz Kafka* by Steven Berkoff (Amber Lane Press 1988). All quotes from the play come from this edition.

Web link

A collection of images from productions of *The Trial* can be found at: http://iainfisher.com/berkoff/berkoff-photo-trial.html

Artaud

> Artaud became a kind of patron saint to all those directors in the 1960s who needed some sort of authority to bless their experimental theatre and 'happenings'.

> In auditioning for the part of a king in a conventional production, Artaud appeared on all fours, barking. This, he explained, was how he viewed the way the king behaved. It is a typical Artaud gesture; however, needless to say, he didn't get the part.

world outside the theatre. He did not want to create productions that could be 'understood'; he wanted to create productions that *helped* the audience to understand.

Artaud thought that theatre should bombard its audience with exaggerated and intense effects. He wanted to use all the technology available to support the performers in confronting the audience with challenging ideas and images. Just as he wanted theatre to exaggerate its effects – through the use of blinding lights, amplified sound and symbolic staging – so he wanted actors to exaggerate their performances. He demanded big gestures and the use of masks, and he asked actors to speak so slowly or quickly that their language became meaningless and merely an auditory effect. He wanted actors to communicate huge emotions and did not wish actors to 'be' their parts. Put simply, his work prioritised metaphor over metonymy.

Directional aims

You will need to develop clear directorial aims for this play. You will need to be able to articulate these aims in a way that a cast would readily be able to understand, and justify and explain them using examples from the text and your own related research. Good directorial aims will, taken as a whole, link the world of the play (in this case, both Kafka's world and Berkoff's version of it) with the world of the audience.

> **Practical exercise**
>
> Present your directorial aims for your imagined production to the rest of your group; this will help you to find the right language and give you practice expressing your ideas clearly and concisely.

While you will need to develop clear ideas about the set, it is worth bearing in mind that Berkoff tends to move away from significant set designs towards a reliance on actors' bodies. Time and again, the play demands the performers to replace the conventional work of the set with mime. For instance, in the office, the 'typists use their heads as typewriters'.

Few things are quite as difficult to create as 'an empty stage'; the emptier the space is, the more significant the slightest object is. A space surrounded on three sides by walls suggests enclosure and imprisonment; a space surrounded on three sides by curtains seems more comfortable, unreal and theatrical; a space surrounded on three sides by an audience sitting on benches has a different effect again. It is not enough to define one's performance space simply as 'an empty space': it needs to be clearly visualised and defined.

Costume

Similarly, the costumes of the characters need to be described precisely. In Berkoff's text, characterisation is kept to a minimum and actors change character – or move from chorus to character – abruptly and frequently. He moves away from the clothing details provided in Kafka's novel, so that his actors are less clearly defined by their costumes. However, wearing an imaginative, stylized costume which corresponds with the metaphorical nature of the text can help an actor immeasurably in realising their role.

> **Further study**
>
> Research the way in which bank workers and minor government officials dressed in Prague and Berlin during the first two decades of the 20th century. This will help you to create costumes for the text; do bear in mind, however, the lack of realism in both Kafka's novel and Berkoff's adaptation.

Reading reviews of past productions of the play can provide insights into how other directors have solved its problems. Take this extract from a review of a production by Scena Theatre, directed by Robert McNamara in Washington DC in 2005:

> Absurdist theatre is director Robert McNamara's terrain and he seems to be having a great deal of fun with the comedy within this stark tragedy. With no backdrops or scrims employed in the production, his cast uses every area of Warehouse Theatre's larger performance venue. In Kimberly Cruce's set we see bare brick walls and an overhead loft space, while on stage are positioned eleven chairs in which the cast sit, clap, type and do other assorted pantomime before jumping up and running around in frenetic activity.
>
> Mr McNamara has paced the play to have a manic energy which suddenly stops, takes a breather and then begins its kinetic ride once more.

Reviews

Web link

Read this review at: www.curtainup.com/trialdc.html

We have already seen that the text can provide us with opportunities for laughter, and that even 'bare brick walls' need to be part of a designed set and not just there by chance.

A review of a production at the Edinburgh Festival Fringe in 1997 includes the following comment:

> The staging is interesting: the acting area is wide but shallow and the trapeze hangs stage right. In the centre is a scaffolding tower on top of which Joseph K. stays for the entire performance. All conversations are held with K. and his interlocutors facing the audience, with one exception: his lover faces him and even mounts the scaffolding with him. Thus are his isolation and alienation emphasised.

Web link

Read this review at: www.britishtheatreguide.info/otherresources/fringe/fringe97-3.htm

It is clear that the set design described above – in many ways a departure from Berkoff's suggestions in the text – is a central feature of the director's aims. The review ends by praising 'a talented cast who have a firm vision of what they want to achieve'; this 'firm vision' is the director's aim which has been clearly communicated and shared with the cast.

Web link

DVDs of Berkoff productions, including *The Trial*, are available from his website: www.stevenberkoff.com.

Our Country's Good

Introduction to the play

Our Country's Good (1988) by Timberlake Wertenbaker is a dramatization of Thomas Keneally's historical novel *The Playmaker* (1987) which describes the first production of a European play – George Farquhar's *The Recruiting Officer* – on the Australian continent. Both Keneally's novel and the play view this event as a symbolic and politically significant moment. They are based upon a true story: historical records indicate that the first dramatic production in Australia was indeed *The Recruiting Officer*, performed in Sydney Cove by an all-convict cast on the King's birthday, 4 June 1789, directed by 2nd Lieutenant Ralph

Thomas Keneally is perhaps best known as the author of *Schindler's Ark* (Coronet 1983), which was adapted into a film directed by Steven Spielberg.

> **Further reading**
>
> You can read more about the historical basis of the novel and play in *The Fatal Shore* by Robert Hughes (Vintage 2003).

Clark. Keneally used journals and other contemporary accounts from the period to develop his material.

The play combines comic, sentimental, tragic and satirical elements, and this variety of moods can pose problems for a director. At heart, however, it is a play about theatre, language and the way in which drama can help individuals 'find their voices'. In this sense, it can be viewed as a political play: drama is shown to be a civilising and civilised endeavour. It contains parallels with the work of a number of the other A2 practitioners: Brecht for its political message and epic quality; Brook for its multiculturalism and hints of spirituality; Grotowski for its focus on the physicality of the characters' loves and their spiritual growth through rehearsal and exploration.

The opening

Poetic realism

The first page of the text establishes exactly what sort of play it is going to be. We are immediately confronted by its poetic realism: the opening image is violent and disturbing, as a man is flogged off stage, while the grim litany of the counted strokes is met with silence by his fellow prisoners in the hold of a transport ship.

We can describe this 'realism' as 'poetic' because it is difficult to imagine the scene being staged in a literal way; the ship's hold does not appear again in the play, so creating a stage set which depicts such a hold realistically would be impractical and unhelpful. Thus, the play immediately places itself within a 'poor theatre' tradition in which complex sets are suggested by gesture and movement rather than by props and set. This is, of course, in harmony with a story about a play that is produced in inhospitable and incommodious conditions.

Language

The language on this first page is hostile, echoing the violence of the image we have been asked to imagine. The use of coarse language in the long, poetic opening speech by Wisehammer confronts the audience with a world they perhaps do not want to share. In their reaction to the convicts' harsh language, the audience may find themselves in alignment with the officers while, at the same time, in light of the flogging, in sympathy with the convicts. Right from the start, they are being asked to see things from two different points of view.

The characters address the audience in a direct and unreal way, again pointing towards a stylized staging. The audience is playing a part in this play. This would be consistent with the views of Brook and Grotowski about the integration of players and audience in the experience of a performance.

The first scene contains a play of sounds – the flogging – and voices; references are arcane or unexplained. If we were to read Keneally's novel, we'd know exactly what Mary is referring to when she says 'I don't know why I did it. Love, I suppose', but as an audience we do not need to know. The mood of her regret and the imprecision of her motivation are clear enough. Wertenbaker appears to have worked with the long speeches in the novel and trimmed them down through improvisation and imagination to distil them to their very essence; nothing superfluous is left.

The play employs a large cast and a relatively large number of scenes for what is, in effect, quite a short play. It is as if Wertenbaker conceives of the play as a dramatic version of a screenplay (which would normally have a large range of locations and lots of short scenes). An intriguing contrast is established between the realism which is conventionally adopted by many films and the impossibility of presenting this play in a theatre in anything like the same way.

Think about...

The first scene is given a rather unusual name: 'The Voyage Out'. Leafing through the play we can see that all of the scenes are given such titles. The second scene has a title almost longer than the scene itself. What should we make of this?

In the second scene, the Aborigine makes a brief and enigmatic appearance. Indeed, the enigma surrounding his character is strengthened by his two later appearances and by the fact that he appears to be suffering from smallpox at the end of the play. What does he symbolise as a character? When we read about the officers shooting native, wild birds and learn that the convicts' smallpox is infecting the indigenous people, we might begin to see a political point emerging about the destructive effects of colonization.

The playwright

Max Stafford-Clark commissioned Wertenbaker to write *Our Country's Good* after he had read Keneally's novel. Both Stafford-Clark and Wertenbaker were working at the Royal Court Theatre in London at the time. Stafford-Clark's idea was to present *Our Country's Good* and Farquhar's *The Recruiting Officer* together, sometimes on alternate nights. He decided to use the same cast and rehearsed both plays at the same time.

It is important to view *Our Country's Good* as part of a larger project (combining a modern, specially written text with a play over 200 years old) which invites both actors and audience to rise to an intellectual and emotional challenge. The fact that the play was presented as part of a joint production sheds light on why *Our Country's Good* ends just as the performance of *The Recruiting Officer* by the convicts begins.

Further reading

Max Stafford-Clark's *Letters to George* (Nick Hern Books 1997) is crucial reading for an account of this process.

Characters

In many ways, *Our Country's Good* is a play of ideas; however, we must not let this stand in the way of characterization. As the play develops, we hear both the officers and convicts, in their different ways, discussing the merits and purpose of the planned production of *The Recruiting Officer*. A successful staging of the play should enable the audience to identify to some extent with all of the characters. The audience should also be able to view the characters as, in part, personifications of the central positions in the play. Phillip, for example, consistently argues for the redemptive and humanizing power of theatre, and the audience is invited to equate his enlightenment with the vision of the dramatist.

In Act 2 scene 2, Phillip says that 'a play is a world in itself'. This forms a corollary with Jacques's famous line in Shakespeare's *As You Like It*: 'all the world's a stage'. Both speakers argue for a close relationship between the stage and the real world.

> **Think about...**
>
> It may seem easy to sympathise with Dabby Bryant, Phillips and Ketch. Why is this? Why is it harder to sympathise, say, with Reverend Johnson? Can we make Johnson into a sympathetic character? How?

> **Think about...**
>
> The transitions made by characters in the play. For instance, Mary Brenham changes from a silent and terrified convict to an articulate and relatively independent young woman, representing the civilizing effects of staging the play. In order to direct *Our Country's Good* and write well about it in the examination, you will need to be able to follow, describe and explain such transitions accurately and precisely.

In talking about the play they are going to stage, the characters examine their own lives. Phillip argues that the ancient Greeks recognized the social value of the theatre and that we should learn from their example. The audience sees the characters as if they are in a laboratory where Phillip's ideas about theatre are being tested. In effect, the play shows us the 'results' of such an experiment, in the way in which key characters come to moderate their extreme behaviour.

As drama students, we are likely to disagree with the military men who dislike and oppose the play. However, to mock their arguments too forcefully or to undermine their points of view through satire would weaken the balance of the play and damage its effectiveness. In the best productions of *Our Country's Good* each character is portrayed vividly and wins the audience's sympathy.

In a way which reflects the discussions of their 'superiors', the convicts have their own debate about the play, which is similarly coloured by their own, very different experiences of society and, in a way, equally prejudiced.

The relationship between Harry and Duckling is important. While unusual, it is a very real form of love which ultimately ends in sadness. Their relationship is not part of the 'drama' argument of the play; instead, through their characters, Wertenbaker dramatises real human emotions which place the production of the convicts' play in a precise, though alien, social context.

Language

Mary Brenham literally 'finds her voice' during the play. Her first line is: '(*inaudibly*) Yes.' Her last line is: 'I love this!'. The movement from the one to the other summarises the movement of the entire play. It's echoed, of course, in other characters, most notably in the character of Liz, who refuses to speak up in her own defence in the belief that to do so would be futile, as she has already lost her individuality and identity. When she is finally persuaded to do so, influenced, it is made clear, by her role in the play, she is able to speak in a formal way echoing the rhythms of speech in *The Recruiting Officer*: 'Your Excellency, I will endeavour to speak Mr Farquhar's lines with the elegance and clarity their own worth commands.'

> Wisehammer's claims that the prologue to Farquhar's play needs rewriting so that it is appropriate to its new context also places an emphasis on language in the play.

The characters reveal their social and geographic origins in the way they speak. There is an obvious difference in *class*, for instance, between the received pronunciation of the senior officers – such as Phillip, Ross and Collins – and the local, lower-class voices of the convicts. Ralph speaks with some affectation – notice his 'euch'. Reverend Johnson has a clergyman's intonation – 'By the grace of God and a belief in the true church, yes'. Campbell has lines which require a comic use of accent – 'Eh, kev, weh, discipline's bad. Very bad'

There is a wide range of accents in the play. Apart from the received pronunciation of the officers, we hear voices from Africa,

Ireland, London, East Anglia, Scotland and Devon. Sideway has a characteristic Cockney twang. Look, for instance, at his long monologue in Act 1 scene 5; it's a marvellous speech full of rhythmic digressions and wonderfully allusive speech patterns, and defines his origins more clearly than any document could do.

Silence and register are also important instruments in this orchestra of voices. Wisehammer's lines are self-consciously poetic at times, while Campbell's inarticulacy mirrors Mary's frightened, Liz's belligerent and Duckling's aggressive silences.

While the wide array of accents can pose problems for the actors, they can also lend themselves to creative casting solutions. In the first production of the play, Jim Broadbent played both Campbell and Arscott; Jude Akuwudike both Tench and the Aboriginal Australian; Ron Cook both Phillip and Wisehammer. The clear distinctions which need to be made in diction, accent, tone and register between these characters make such 'doubling-up' dramatically feasible.

> So confident was the company in the significance of *voice* in the production that a number of female actors took male parts. While this underlines the 'poetic realism' in the play it also makes clear that the *voice* of a character – rather than physical appearance or facial features – is the defining element of their presentation.

According to dialect designer and coach Paul Meier:

> It is a particularly challenging play dialectally, in that many of the characters are also players in *The Recruiting Officer*, and need to assume or attempt the dialects appropriate to their roles; and in that *Our Country's Good* is a play about language, its uses and abuses, and calls for moment-to-moment dialect modification as characters pursue their objectives, conscious of 'code-switching' as a stratagem for achieving them.
>
> A character's dialect will help us identify him/her, but some characters will slip across identities as they negotiate new roles and new possibilities for themselves.

Web link

www.kutheatre.com/03-04_season/ OurCountry'sGoodDramaturg'.html

Learning to speak gives the convicts more than just a voice: they realise their potential as human beings. There is less to divide them now from the ruling classes. Finding a voice, they are able to find themselves as a new community.

Directorial aims

Our Country's Good, as we have noted, has an essentially cinematic form: 22 short scenes in two acts, with leaps of time and place made between them like camera cuts. How could the play be staged without making it look like a third-rate film?

> The role of the Aboriginal Australian may be to show that not only Europeans but European language (specifically English) has now colonized the continent.

Should a realistic approach be adopted? Considering that the play is about individuals, spiritual voice and language, a realistic depiction of indigenous Australian flora, the holds of ships and rowing boats may distract from these themes. Alternatively, you could draw from the work of Grotowski and experiment to find out just how *little* is needed in the way of props, imagery and sound to create each location; experiment with the scene titles themselves: can they be read aloud or presented on placards in a Brechtian way? How can we use their rather whimsical humour?

In a group, try creating the hold of a transport ship using your bodies. You are the convicts; create the impression of being in the oppressed confines of a vessel. Begin the first scene in such a way, and add the off-stage voice and the sound effects of the flogging. Do you need the sound of the sea and creaking timbers or can you rely on the 'brutal physicality' of your own acting?

Try staging Act 1 scene 7. It's a key scene in the play as a whole, and your solutions to staging it will inform your staging of the entire play. Do you need water on stage? Do you need a boat and oars? Perhaps the convicts, in rehearsal, could use whatever props come to hand (a piece of wood for a fan, for example). What is the *minimum* you need to make this scene work?

Think about...

There is a wide range of moods in the play. Some scenes are tragic and sad, some moving, others comic or even sentimental; several are bitingly satirical; some combine at least two or three of these moods. Go through the text assigning 'mood' words to each scene.

Think about how you can move smoothly from one scene to another, when the location, timescale and mood significantly alters. Practise using unusual staging strategies, subtle lighting, music and sound effects, reading the scene headings aloud, and so on. Once you've tried all of these things, start paring them away. Do you really need the sound of a didgeridoo? The cry of cockatoos? Gunshots? Do you really need to flick the lighting across the stage? Does reading out the scene heading amuse the cast but confuse the audience? What happens when you leave it out?

In the first scene of the play, it seems as if the speeches have been pared down to their bare minimum, perhaps as a result of Wertenbaker's workshops with the cast, experimenting and improvising from the novel. Try to adopt this same approach with all of the production values in the play: start big and then see just how much you can leave out.

Humour

For a play with such a serious subject, *Our Country's Good* contains a surprising and varied amount of humour:

> In Act 1 scene 5 Meg contributes darkly humorous wit to the auditions. This element of **black humour** is something we may expect from a play about convicts.

> In Act 2 scene 1 there's another successful piece of comic action: 'Because it's not a compass... It's a piece of paper with north written on it.'

> In Act 1 scene 5, when asked if she can read, Dabby tells Ralph: 'Not those marks in books... I can read dreams very well.' Although Wertenbaker is developing the key idea here

Think about...

Even the stage directions have a certain wit: '*Meg Long is very old and very smelly*'. You may have tried acting old before, but have you ever tried acting *smelly*?

about finding civilisation through language, she is also giving the actor a humorous line which will work well on stage.

The play is about the theatre and it also contains some fine jokes about actors and acting:

- Sideway's absurdly melodramatic style is mocked in Act 1 scene 11 in a way reminiscent of Bottom in *A Midsummer Night's Dream*

- Wisehammer's improvised kiss in Act 2 scene 7 has an anachronistically modern feel to it.

- Act 2 scene 7 contains some delightful confusion when, during the squabbling about the rehearsal and casting, Mary says, tetchily: 'You can't play a man, Dabby … in the play I know I'm a woman, whereas if you played Kite, you would have to think you were a man.' Apart from the wit of this line of argument itself, there is also irony in the fact that in the first production, the actor playing Mary, a woman, also played the part of Reverend Johnson, a man, and the actor playing Dabby, another woman, also took the role of William Faddy.

> You might choose to persist with the cross-casting and doubling up of the first production in order to invigorate the humour of this scene.

The play was first performed in the late 1980s. In many ways, it is a protest against the policies of Margaret Thatcher's Conservative government in the United Kingdom. This was a period of soaring inflation, which hit the poorest hardest, and of relatively high unemployment. The Conservative government argued for harsh penalties and increased sentencing of offenders. Many left-wing critics of Thatcher's government deplored her attitude to the poorest members of society, who were in practical ways disenfranchised and marginalised, and their voices silenced.

Social context

Thatcher's government prioritised a free market economy over state funding. The play is in tune with her left-wing critics who argued that the theatre – which in many cases requires state subsidies to be viable – is an important tool in creating and civilising society.

Thatcher also achieved notoriety in the 1980s for her stance on the Falklands War. In sending a task force to fight the Argentineans, she reawoke the guilt of a colonial power. This resonates in *Our Country's Good*; for instance, there is contemporary irony in Wisehammer's discarded prologue: 'We left our country for our country's good.'

Think about…

Thatcher notoriously said that 'There's no such thing as society. There are individual men and women, and there are families.' Consider exactly what happens when you apply that opinion to this play!

Coram Boy

Introduction to the play

Coram Boy is a novel for children written by Jamila Gavin and published in 2000, when it won the Whitbread Children's Book of the Year. The play, adapted by Helen Edmundson from Gavin's book, was first produced in 2005 at the National Theatre, London.

The story combines fact and fiction. The narrative of Coram's Foundling Hospital in London is a true one. Thomas Coram had made money as a seaman in the early 18th century and on

> The Whitbread judges called the book 'an engrossing historical novel with life well beyond the pages of the book and superb narrative control over complex stories.'

Further study

If you're able to, make a visit to Coram's Fields, between Bloomsbury and Islington in north central London. The park was once the site of the Foundling Hospital, whose museum containing music manuscripts and artworks, is nearby.

Further reading

Coram Boy adapted by Helen Edmundson (Nick Hern Books 2005).

his return to London established the Foundling Hospital for the city's street children. He had powerful friends who helped him in this project, one of whom was the painter and caricaturist William Hogarth (although he does not feature in the play). Hogarth contributed paintings to the hospital, and it became in practice the first public art gallery in the city. Another important friend of Coram's was the composer George Frideric Handel (who does feature). Annual performances of Handel's Messiah – a Christmas oratorio – provided regular income for the charity. One such performance is recreated in both the novel and the play.

Directorial aims

In some ways, *Coram Boy* seems to be influenced by screenwriting: when we read it, it can seem as if we are reading a film script rather than a play. Helen Edmundson makes mention of this in her introduction. She recognises that 'the scenes, which are often short, need to flow or tumble in and out of each other – sometimes even overlap'.

Edmundson also tells us in this introduction that the original production used the full resources of the National Theatre's Olivier Theatre with its revolving stage and that the angel in the play was able to fly realistically. But she says there was a limit to the resources used: 'There were no grand sets, no tricks, no trap doors, no water features.' 'The stage demands,' she says, 'were met by the actors, and by the lighting.'

Melodrama

In many ways the play is written in the tradition of melodrama. Melodrama has a rather poor reputation today, but it should not be dismissed out of hand. It was a popular dramatic form in England in the mid to late 19th century. Its origins lie in the anomalous licensing laws of the day, which limited plays to a few, censored theatres, but which allowed music concerts to be more widely and freely performed. Melodrama began by mixing a full musical score with dramatic interludes. In this way, the theatre managers claimed the performances were musical and exempt from the theatrical licensing rules.

In subject matter and style, melodramas were sensational and controversial. Murder, riot, sexual assaults and so on were their staple diet. The subject matter of *Coram Boy* has certainly much in common with Victorian melodrama. Moreover, many melodramas were themselves adaptations of popular novels.

> A particularly successful melodrama of the 19th century presented a version of Elizabeth Gaskell's *Mary Barton*, for example.

The theatres which produced melodrama used extraordinarily complex stage machinery and part of the thrill for the audience lay in watching such effects. One play, which included the rescue of a drowning woman, used wooden waves stretched as low flats across the stage. Three actresses, identically dressed, bobbed up and down in turn from trapdoors in the stage floor. Combined with lighting effects and loud music, the effect captivated the audience, giving the impression of the heroine tossed beneath the waves by the power of the storm.

Often, melodrama dealt with social and political issues. Some of the most successful dealt with social problems resulting from the industrial revolution. These plays often began with a dramatisation of the social problems: greedy mill-owners, poor working conditions, poverty, and so on, leading to strikes and discord. The story would then gradually focus more closely on one relationship – for instance, the love between a strike leader and the daughter of a mill owner. The issues of the play – such as the conflict between workers and employers – would intervene in the love affair. In the end, the lovers, against the odds, would attain a happy ending.

It is important when working with *Coram Boy* to recognise that its characterisation must be as subtle as possible. How can we generate sympathy for a character such as Otis Gardiner? The plot must also be a vehicle for sensitive stagecraft and the development of real relationships – as it was in the best Victorian melodramas.

> Critics of melodramas have observed that they begin with a social problem but end not with the resolution of that initial problem (working conditions and poverty, for instance) but of the emergent personal problem (in this example, the marriage of the two lovers). *Coram Boy* works like this too. The happy ending is a happy ending to a lovers' relationship; the initial social problem of illegitimacy, foundlings and murder is left unresolved.

Brecht and epic theatre

If you studied Brecht as part of your AS course, you might like to use some of his approaches when working on *Coram Boy*. Brecht responded to the popular, melodramatic traditions of European theatre – the traditions which Peter Brook in *The Empty Space* (Penguin 2008) calls 'rough theatre' – by developing a more politically explicit storytelling genre, which came to be known as **epic theatre**.

In Brecht's theatre, the narrator became a central figure, relating a story that was enacted in front of the audience. The **fourth wall** – so important in realism – vanished. New mechanical advances allowed for the use of projection in theatre: images that reflected upon the action on stage could be shown behind the actors, providing a new perspective on the story that allowed for modern or historical parallels to be drawn.

In the 1920s, Brecht collaborated with the director Erwin Piscator. It was Piscator who first used the term 'epic theatre', which for him meant the inclusion of film in a theatrical performance, such as newsreel clips and cartoons. Piscator also made use of narration, music and multiple settings, which were to become staple elements of Brecht's work. These added social and historical background, focusing the spectator on the political messages behind the performance.

In brief, Brechtian theatre can be defined as any form of theatre that puts a social or political message before the exploration of character. In planning a production of *Coram Boy*, it might benefit a director to look at such an approach.

Staging

There is no question that *Coram Boy* presents problems of staging. A simple reading of the opening page is enough:

> *MESHAK begins his journey down the south aisle. He feels that he shouldn't be in the cathedral, and it takes him all his courage to dare to move forward – past the gargoyles and the bloody crucifixion scenes.*

It will not help to spend too long in the examination suggesting solutions for all of the staging issues relating to *Coram Boy*. You must guard against turning the examination answer into purely an issue of stage management. For instance, you could deal with the stage direction above by responding to the scenic issues it raises, or you could look at the characterisation of Meshak, whose fear and uncomprehending awe become a motif for his behaviour. An audience should sympathise with him, even when he is revealed as complicit in the murder of babies.

On the other hand, a good student must show some understanding of staging issues. You need to present a clear overview of the guiding principles you would use for staging; you can then work on just one or two examples of staging problems in the set extract. Make sure that you cover them in sufficient detail to demonstrate a sensitive and imaginative understanding of the problems raised by the text and possible solutions.

Think about...

Both melodrama and epic theatre – in different ways – use contemporary technology to help with staging. It might therefore be appropriate to use similarly contemporary staging devices in your planned production; these might include a more ambitious use of digital projectors and sophisticated sound effects.

Casting is also an issue to be addressed. Performers in the play need to be able to sing. In the first production, the parts of the young Alexander Ashbrook and his son Aaron later in the play were both taken by Anna Madeley. The musical power of the production is of course one of its strengths and a good director will need a good music director to work with. You may wish to refer to this relationship in answers on the play.

You might like to think about the links between Coram's Foundling Hospital and the painter William Hogarth. Looking at Hogarth's works – his formal portraits and his more caricatured narrative sequences such as *The Rake's Progress* – might provide a designer with insightful ideas about staging and set design.

In the 1980s, the National Theatre in London staged a series of successful promenade performances. The plays presented in this manner, directed by Bill Bryden, included Tony Harrison's versions of the English medieval mystery plays, *The Passion* and an adaptation of Flora Thompson's *Lark Rise* by Keith Dewhurst. *Lark Rise* used the promenade form – where the audience become spectators and are free to walk around the floor of an open area within which sets are constructed or spaces left free – to present a fast-moving sequence of short scenes in complex settings. This is exactly the problem we have to address with *Coram Boy*.

Grotowski and poor theatre

In the tradition of poor theatre, as advocated by Jerzy Grotowski and others, the emphasis is placed on the actor – on emotions and personal relationships – and not on set or costume. A prospective director of *Coram Boy* may like to look at this tradition to gain inspiration for their own production.

The phrase 'poor theatre' is tied closely to Grotowski's work; to understand this term fully is to understand Grotowski's approach to drama. Grotowski defined theatre as 'what takes place between spectator and actor' and he felt that the key role of a director was to employ, explore and develop the 'special demands' placed on each of these parties during performance. He believed that audiences needed to be shocked by a performance into discovering their own 'psychic layers'. He rejected the rational, artificial or hackneyed in working practices.

Grotowski argued that every new production should be a new 'experiment in some aspect of the actor/audience relationship'. When this is taken as the cornerstone of theatre, the priorities we are used to when evaluating, understanding and devising a production are transformed. Gone is a concern for decorative setting and costume, and a historic respect for text or for straightforward stories and meanings. In their place is a theatre in which the actor is a 'holy' figure leading the audience through a psychological and spiritual experience, so as to liberate their responses from the conventional and the hackneyed.

> Grotowski also rejected the premise that the first duty of a theatre is to produce plays!

Grotowski's actors replaced many elements of traditional theatre with their own bodies, presenting a refined and brutal physicality to the audience. His working methods gradually became more focused on this physical element of an actor's work.

Acting

Finally, the play is more likely to fail through weak and unprepared acting than it is through shortcomings in set and design. A director must therefore develop strategies for bringing the characters to life. It is important not to view characters too simplistically: don't neglect the 'good' side of apparently 'bad' characters nor the 'bad' side of the apparently 'good'. At the heart of the play is a complex morality. Trying to win some degree of sympathy from the audience for *all* of the characters may be a demanding directorial aim; however, it would be an interesting one and would serve the play well.

Devised Drama

Key features

This unit accounts for 20% of the overall A-level mark and is allocated a total of 80 marks (fewer than those available for Unit 3).

You must work as part of a team in this unit. You will be in a group of between two to eight acting candidates, with up to five design candidates and, if you wish, one directing candidate.

Each piece must include a minimum of two actors and no more than one director, nor more than one designer in each field.

The piece must run for between 15 and 40 minutes; large groups will require more time and smaller groups, less.

> It is permitted to include a non-examinee to help with certain technical aspects of a performance or, rarely, as performers when the centre has an entry of only one candidate. All of this is explained further in the specification.

What have I got to do?

For this part of your course, you have to do the following:

➤ Present for an audience a devised drama which should realise clear dramatic intentions.

➤ Prepare, develop and present this piece as part of a group. To be successful, there must be a real sense of creative cooperation throughout this process. However, you must choose a particular performance skill that you will demonstrate yourself. This can be acting, of course, or directing, but it can also be any one of the following design skills:

➤ Costume design and construction

➤ Stage design

➤ Mask design

➤ Lighting and/or sound design

➤ Demonstrate your knowledge and understanding of these skills, your ability to employ them, and your readiness to experiment with them to develop and improve them.

> Students must present a production or performance in a chosen theatrical style, 'underpinned by independent thought and refined in the light of their research'.

You have a free choice regarding the subject matter of your devised drama, but it needs to be harmonious with your chosen dramatic style. The choice of style is also completely free, and although the specification lists suggestions (including naturalism, epic theatre, theatre of cruelty and docu-theatre) the list is just there for guidance; you can follow your own interests.

This part of the course requires a minimum of ten weeks' work. We recommend that you read through all of the following sections before starting work on your piece; you can then revisit them when you need to during your preparation and rehearsal period.

Assessment

There are three areas of assessment:

- Preparation and development
- Supporting notes
- Presentation of the finished piece.

The first two elements account for a total of 30 marks available (out of the maximum of 80) and the performance itself is marked out of 50.

Preparation and development

The mark you receive for this element will be derived from the monitoring of your work by your teacher. There are three key areas that you will be marked on.

Firstly, you have to make clear your understanding of your chosen dramatic style and adhere to it sensibly and sensitively throughout the process. This chosen style will influence your topic, theme and material, and will shape the dramatic intentions you have for your audience.

You need to define a style - through research and experience – not simply in performance terms, but also regarding the expected subject matter, the themes and the relationship with an audience. In a naturalist play, for example, we would expect to see a significant narrative involving environment and character which is told through revelatory moments and carefully constructed dialogue; we would expect characters to develop and interact with some emotion; we would expect largely realistic sets and we would expect no direct attention to the audience. In choosing to devise a piece in a 'naturalistic' style, we are choosing all of this. It is therefore best to be clear from the start what you are choosing!

Your teacher may guide you towards a certain style based on the work you have done and the productions you have been able to see, or you may be left a little more to your own devices. You need to make this first important decision carefully and in a well-informed way. But you must not waste time dithering. Think carefully. Do some general research. Discuss your options frankly, and consider the strengths and weaknesses of the group's skills. Decide wisely and then stick to your decision.

Secondly, during the preparation and rehearsal process, you have to be inventive, creative and co-operative. Work as a team. Listen to one another's suggestions and ask questions thoughtfully (rather than aggressively or confrontationally).

Make sure that you are explicit in linking the work you have done on the course, and the plays you have seen especially, with what you are devising. The examination board call this unit 'synoptic', and they are expecting to see in it the fruits of all your study in drama.

The emphasis during the preparation time is on group work. It is possible that you will want to go on and apply for a drama course in further or higher education. Increasingly often, universities and colleges are asking applicants to take part in short group exercises as part of the selection process. Your work in this unit will help you towards this.

Thirdly, you will also be assessed on your own individual skills. So, alongside your group work, you must not neglect developing and rehearsing your own part.

Supporting notes

Just under a third of the marks for this unit are reserved for the preparation and development of your piece and for the supporting notes.

The golden rule for achieving a high mark for your notes is to manage them from day one. Retrospective notes – scribbled down during the last few possible days when you should be concentrating on your performance – will inevitably gain low marks as well as distracting you from your performing. Think of your work as a notebook, a diary or a series of experimental jottings. Make it interesting rather than polished, exploratory rather than conclusive, a collage rather than a painting. It should be a sketchbook for your finished performance.

> Your notes should outline *your* role in the development of the performance piece. If you find one day that you have too little to add to your notes, maybe this is because you are contributing too little to the group's work.

Again, there are three elements to the assessment:

1. Your supporting notes should be explicit in referring to the research and exploration you have undertaken in relation to the chosen style, and you should include express remarks about productions seen. You will need to use specialist terminology in doing so, which will make some of your notes read like an essay. You will also need to articulate your dramatic intentions. (Are you trying to make your audience laugh at themselves? Sympathise with others? Are you challenging wide-held prejudices? And so on.)

2. As you develop the work, your notes will reflect your progress and include evaluation and refinement of ideas.

3. Finally, you will assess the piece in terms of its adopted style and as a piece in its own right.

You will also reflect on your own performance. You will probably have acted in the piece, but you might have chosen to direct or to design an element of the work. Your supporting notes will trace accurately your individual progress.

Acting

If you are focusing on acting in the final piece, you should give details of your approach to performance skills, and describe your experiments with techniques and the work you've done to build a character. Think about the following questions:

- How has your chosen theatrical style contributed to your own acting approaches and style?

- What research have you undertaken?

- What skills have you had to work on?

- What rehearsal techniques have you used?

- What advice have you been given?

- How useful was it?

- How have the ideas from your theory units helped you here?

> The following pages give some suggestions about how you might go about doing this.

If you intend to be assessed as a designer for the final piece, your notes should include relevant sketches, diagrams and photographs. If you decide to focus on costume design, you may wish to include samples of materials or dyes used; if you focus on stage settings you will need to produce a scale model of the set for the group piece. Lighting and sound designers must include lists of the equipment and accessories used, as well as things like cue sheets and plot sheets. Whatever aspect of design you look at, you'll need to include a personal evaluation of the creative cooperation of the group as well as a self-assessment. You'll evaluate the successful development of the project against its original aims (you will have developed and modified your design proposals as the project grows). You also need to show a thorough awareness of health and safety factors and their implications for your work.

The examiners advise you that although there is no prescribed format for the notes, they should be written in an appropriate tone, using specialist terminology where necessary. They should be approximately 2,000 words in length. While you shouldn't waste your time counting words, remember that length does not necessarily equal quality; your notes should be relevant and well-organised.

While the notes should form a working book, they should also be legible and logical, of course, because someone else has to read them. They should offer an insight into your thoughts and ideas as the original piece progresses and clarify precisely the links between your chosen theatrical style and your performance. They should show that the final piece of theatre is the result of intellectual rigour and artistic sensitivity, and not just a collection of shaky audition pieces put together by instinct and luck.

High-grade notes

The examination board has published some guidance concerning the qualities of high-grade notes. It is useful to unpick their instructions and see exactly what they mean:

Aims and objectives

> The dramatic aims and objectives of the group will be precisely defined.

Design factors

A clear idea about aims and objectives is just as important for the design of your piece as it is for its content and style. Different stage layouts create different relationships with the audience. How do your aims affect the relationship between performers and audience? How will your choice of staging contribute to achieving these aims? Do you have a designer in your team who will lead in these areas, or will the group be sharing responsibility?

Your **aims** are the big and abstract ideas behind the piece you produce. Maybe you want to confront the audience with a moral dilemma; maybe you want to explore the effect of a tragic accident on a family or depict the effect of big social changes on a small community; maybe you want to show the spiritual journey of a young man.

Your **objectives**, on the other hand, are smaller. You may want to entertain your audience by creating realistic dialogue and psychologically convincing characters; puzzle them with shocking and violent images; or amuse them with humour and humorous situations.

You'll notice that the question 'why?' is still lurking under these aims and objectives. It's a question worth asking. *Why* do you want to confront the audience with a tragic dilemma? For their own good? In order for you to have a better idea about the function of tragedy? In order for you and the audience to understand the genre of tragedy better? By asking such questions you will be able to clarify your aims and refine your objectives. If you think through these questions properly when you look at your objectives and ask why, you'll find yourself going back to your initial aims.

You'll also see that your aims will tend to be abstract and intellectual, whereas your objectives will be practical and concrete. Use your notes to make notes; thinking about your aims and objectives cannot really be finished at the first discussion. As you undertake research and experimentation, you'll find yourselves amending your objectives, even if your aims remain firm.

The 'pursuit of excellence' – that phrase is a key one, isn't it? Your notes should naturally describe what you've done, but they should also contain your thoughts on how to make it better, and how to achieve your objectives as effectively and as purely as possible.

Design factors

Different theatre styles require different styles of acting as well as different styles of design. As you clarify the shape and form of your piece, you must clarify how the design of it will contribute to its effect.

Although your notes should offer more than just a diary, there is a diary element to them which should enable you to engage with the developing piece. They will show your understanding of what you are doing well, where you are meeting your own personal objectives, and where you are not quite succeeding. Be objective about your successes and honest about your limitations. This will help you feel good about what you can do and also help you to focus on areas where things aren't perfect, where you might need to seek advice or undertake further exploration.

Let's look at another piece of guidance from the examination board specification:

> The notes will be presented logically and will be well written in an appropriate register using specialist terminology accurately and with confidence.

An appropriate register

> 'An appropriate register' is like saying 'in a suitable tone of voice'. It means the style is right.

'An appropriate register' is a flexible phrase. A collection of notes is not a polished essay. But it isn't a series of illegible jottings either. The following suggestions should help you to write up your day's work, and show you how to make your notes and speculations readable:

- Don't be afraid to write questions as well as answers. Often, improving your ability to ask the right question is the easiest way to finding the best answer.

- You are an actor, designer and director – you are no longer a student! You should adopt the language and concepts of the theatre. Your notes should be as professional a piece of work as you can possibly make them.

- It's useful to think of your notes as a notebook or sketchbook. So, buy a decent notebook or an artist's sketchbook to use. Visit the art department in your school or college and look at the ways in which art students use their sketchbooks to prepare for their own examination pieces; this is what you should be doing in your notes.

> A4 artists' sketchbooks are not cheap, but they are worth every penny. They feel good to use, the paper is excellent, and there is a real sense of accomplishment in using one.

- Use your sketchbook in a versatile way. If you make jottings during a rehearsal, glue them in. Add a comment or two. You might find a photograph in a magazine or newspaper, or a postcard at an art gallery, that somehow sums up just the mood or image you're after: glue it in with a comment. You might have a series of digital photographs from a research visit or a rehearsal – stick them in with a commentary.

Your final notes should be informative, coherent and easily understood.

Health and safety

You need to show in your notes (and during your performance, of course) that you are aware of the health and safety issues involved in staging your piece. You need to be specific here, examining the precise health and safety implications thrown up by your piece, rather than being too general. Your teacher will help you identify what these are. However, the following are some general ideas to consider, to give you an idea of what sort of things you should be aware of, and to help you rehearse and perform safely and responsibly.

- Behave in a responsible manner when working in practical study situations

- Wear clothing that is appropriate for practical drama work

- All studios should have notices of fire exits and equipment

- Naked flames must not be used in performance without prior consultation

- Check carefully before standing on chairs or rostra to make sure that they are on flat surfaces, stable, and able to take your weight

- When rehearsing fight sequences, make sure that you carefully rehearse the moves that make up the sequence in slow motion until you are sure mistakes will not be made; always agree on a start signal so that no one is surprised

- When engaging in any vigorous activity, warm your body up with gentle exercise; sudden or strong movements when you're cold can cause injury

- Do not attempt heavy lifting; learn how to lift and bend properly

- All set and scenery must be carefully secured with attention to balance and top-heavy construction

- Cables should not cross any walkways unless they are fully taped and covered

- Powered equipment, particularly lanterns, generate heat; do not place such items in closed areas, nor near inflammable materials, nor in a place where people can come into contact with them

- In the case of stage lighting, rigging should be done without the power on.

A word of warning

As your notes near conclusion, you need to look over them to make sure that they are a coherent whole. It may be a good idea, in the end, to use your notebook as the basis for a well-organised, typed-up 2,000-word piece. You need to make sure that a new reader will make sense of your work and intentions. Of course, you should submit your scrapbook too, as a sort of appendix to your summary.

As we have said, there will be a diary element to your notes. The whole point of them is to trace the development of your ideas, after all. However, you must avoid a blandly descriptive diary which offers no interpretation. An entry such as: 'Monday. We rehearsed the first scene. It went well. The lights did not work very well' is not helpful!

Time management

Planning

At your first meeting, draw up a calendar that outlines the time your group will spend on each element of the preparation and rehearsal period, and show precisely when you will do the work. As a broad scenario, there are three sections to this work, and it is as well not to confuse them:

1. Research and plan your piece, establishing aims and objectives and a basic shape and theme.

2. Complete a script with a detailed scenario that turns your ideas into something concrete.

3. Rehearse your script for performance.

Try not to mix these up. It is a bad sign if you're still not sure what your aims and objectives are when you have a script, and it is also a bad sign if you are still making whole-scale revisions to your script once you have entered the final rehearsal period. It's pretty disastrous, too, if your design team is not working closely in step with your acting team. Don't leave technical elements to the end.

You have to be honest with yourselves. You will not get everything done in the minimum time if you want to do it well. You need to build emergency sessions into your calendar. Don't just schedule them at the end of the process: setting yourselves clear deadlines for each stage of the process is good practice.

You must all cooperate as a group. If, when the calendar is being drawn up, it becomes obvious that members of your group are hindering progress through a reluctance to commit themselves to dates and times, you must resolve this straight away. This is one of the very few occasions in your school or college life where the quality of your cooperation is assessed. Do not let your team down!

Suggested schedule

We recommend the following programme for preparing and developing your piece. A more detailed look at some of the individual stages can be found on later pages.

Planning, researching, shaping	**1. Considering a theatrical style** Your chosen theatrical style is going to influence every element of your piece, so this choice needs to be made carefully and in a well-informed way. Talk clearly about what you have read, plays you have performed and seen. **2. Improvisation and experimentation** Bring ideas back to the group. Explore some of them through improvisation and see what you find. This takes time, but you must be disciplined – do not spend too long experimenting. **3. Shaping a scenario** At this stage, you should be able to draft a scenario for your piece. What's going to happen? How will it be structured and shaped? Where are the climaxes? How does the pace quicken and slow? How should the audience react at each key moment? You should be able to clarify precisely the objectives which have flowed from your aim. Having your scenario set down clearly is important and it is essential that each member of the group has a copy of this. **4. Discussing the whole** This is where you integrate acting ideas and design ideas: how will stage, set, style, costume, mask and language gel together (or strike against one another)? You might want to have a look at the work of Gordon Craig to give you some ideas here. There will be plenty to write in your notes as you set out the shape and the form of your piece.

Preparing a script	**5. The script** Once you've set yourselves clear aims and objectives, and once you've designed a shape for your piece, you can get down to the nitty-gritty of devising scenes and speeches.
Preparing a performance	**6. Rehearsal** Rehearsal is not the same process as devising. You should now have a script. You will make some changes. There may be some cuts, maybe the odd rewrite. But the script you're holding is basically the script you're going to perform. You've moved to a new stage now: preparing a performance. Imagine how long a company would have working with a script. You have maybe three weeks! Do not pretend you're rehearsing when really you're rewriting and going over old ground pointlessly. Stick to your schedule! **7. Run-throughs and previews** Don't let the exam be the first time you've performed the piece for an audience. Perform it to another group of students – maybe the AS group – so that you get a feel for the thing in performance and so you can get a response from an intelligent audience. You can also sort out technical gremlins. An evening performance for parents and teachers is also an excellent plan. Set this date right at the start and keep to it. The purpose of previews is to cast a critical eye over the piece. You may still want to make changes, maybe to the pace or to the lighting plot, or maybe to one or two speeches where there have been specific problems. While organising a preview is valuable, it will be rendered pointless if you haven't built in time to evaluate it and make modifications. (This provides more material for the notes, of course.) **8. Last revisions and dress rehearsal** The dress rehearsal is not a preview. It's a last opportunity to check everything works, and to check that everyone is ready to do their best. Ignore the superstition which claims that when the dress rehearsal is poor, the show will be a hit: if the dress rehearsal is poor, you've got a problem. Do your very best. Then do it again for the exam.

Let's now break some of these key areas down and look at them in more detail.

Planning, researching and shaping

Research

Research is important: the ability to undertake good research and use the results relevantly is one way of ensuring success in this unit. Research enables you to turn abstract ideas into concrete drama. Once you've settled on an idea that relates to your chosen theatre style, draw up a list of research areas to share around the group. Then meet again after the research period – which needs to be short and concentrated – and review your tentative plans in the light of what you've seen and found out.

Good research will help you come up with interesting ideas. You might make a series of visits to gain information and insights. Such visits might also furnish you with the raw material for key speeches.

In his work with David Hare on *The Permanent Way*, a play that deals with the political, social and personal issues emerging from the decision to privatise British Rail, in a genre which is probably best called 'docu-drama', the director Max Stafford-Clark encouraged his cast to undertake considerable research. He described this process as folows:

> There was no script at this point, just a list of phone numbers and contacts with people who had been involved at different levels in the railway industry. We met bankers and civil servants involved in the original privatisation. We talked to several directors of major train operating companies. We talked to the bereaved and survivors of train crashes. Some of the actors spent time working as ticket collectors, clad in train uniforms; and others observed and talked to a track gang for several days. Everybody was happy to talk and keen to tell their story. At the start of each day, we would each report our encounters to the whole group. From these stories and these meetings David crafted this compelling play.

One research technique involved the actors interviewing key figures and then recreating the interview back at base for the rest of the cast. The actor would adopt the role and, as far as possible, voice and stance of the person interviewed and then give his testimony, answering questions and so on, improvising a character that had become fictional, but was based on scrupulous research.

Use your notes to record your research, whether as a written account or as something more visual, such as photographs or diagrams. Good research is a test of your observational skills. Don't be afraid to stare! What's going on in those other motorway cars? What are those women actually talking about? Don't be afraid to speculate, either. Using your imagination to juxtapose and develop observed scenes is really a cornerstone in drama. Look closely at your raw material, and then ask yourself 'what happens next?' and try to come up with a convincing answer. It doesn't have to be observed scenes, either. Look through a set of local newspapers and cut out any interesting or relevant stories.'

Design factors

Take care when researching using 'real' props. If your set requires a telephone box, making arrangements with BT to provide you with a dummy one is clever, but means that everything else in your set must have a similar degree of realism. The same argument applies to costume: it may not work dramatically for actors to wear realistic costumes. Exaggeration or stylization may achieve more appropriate effects. You have to think about this (and record your debate and decisions in your notes).

Web link

More on the creation of *The Permanent Way*, see the play's website at www.outofjoint.co.uk/prods/permanentway.html

Observation

Conflict

Some people will tell you that drama is founded on conflict: a conflict of personalities, politics, culture or values, mood or atmosphere. Good research should give you the grounding for the form of your piece, for the language in which it will be voiced, and for the conflicts that will create its drama.

Art as inspiration

Maybe your idea doesn't lend itself to the kind of research where you can visit places and listen to real people. Maybe you have an idea you want to work with, but you can't find anything concrete to help you work on it. Perhaps you have chosen a style and you have a clear idea of theme but you need something which will give you a setting or a scenario. Sometimes, an afternoon spent leafing through books of paintings and photographs can throw up fascinating scenarios which will help solve this dilemma. Artaud, in *Theatre and its Double*, writes about how he was fascinated by the painting in the Louvre of *Lot and his Daughters*. He could see the drama implicit in the painting, and in his imagination could see a way of transforming the painting into a performance.

Web link

Go to www.museumwales.ac.uk/art/online and search for 'Sinnott' under 'Artist'.

Visit the website of the National Museums and Galleries of Wales. In their catalogue you will find an image of a painting called *Running away with the Hairdresser* by Kevin Sinnott, which is held in the National Museum, Cardiff. Look at it closely. Think about it. Who are these characters (and which one is the hairdresser)? Where have they come from and where are they going? You can ask more questions along these lines and then move on to explore your starting point a little more elaborately. For example, what kind of mood is suggested by the painting? Is it a happy one or a sad one? A lonely one or an erotic one? How does the detail in the background contribute to the effect of the painting?

Design factors

Designers too can get plenty of ideas from works of art. David Hockney is just one of many modern painters who have made significant contributions to set design and mood setting.

Finally, ask yourself the big questions. What does the painting mean? Is there any significance in the way the couple is running from the light into the shade? How do you read the gesture which is placed right in the centre of the painting? Is the gap between the hands growing or closing? What are the conflicts implicit here?

Hazards

When you are preparing material in this way, here's a short list of dos and don'ts to consider. They are not set in stone, but you should think about them carefully.

You may want to consider the advantages and disadvantages of using video recordings of your rehearsals. Watching them back can be helpful, especially for listening back to dialogue.
Remember, though, that it's not a professionally filmed and edited recording and you're not on TV! Try not to be distracted by technical shortcomings and focus on what you're seeing as theatre.

Watch less television. This sounds absurd, but maybe it isn't so mad. Television drama has very different qualities from theatre. You might be amazed to know just how many sixth-form group productions try to ape television genres and forms. Chat shows, soaps, talent competitions and stand-up comedy are not the kind of things we should be dealing with here, and it would be difficult to imagine any devised drama which was able to pull off the incorporation of this kind of performance into the production. Anything which belongs on television should, quite simply, stay there.

Watch fewer films. Similarly, films use all sorts of techniques that do not transfer well to the theatre. Because the camera can cut away suddenly from a conversation, for example, short scenes can be very effective. In a theatre, where we have to concern ourselves with exits and entrances as well as with voice projection and stage presence, a short, intimate dialogue which cuts away to another scene can be cumbersome in performance and pretty unconvincing. Good theatre comes from the use of a language, as Artaud observed, which is uniquely theatrical. Film acting is a very different kind of skill.

See more theatre. It's obvious, really, that if you are going to devise an effective piece of original drama you need to be as familiar as possible with drama in performance. Maybe you've seen some high-budget, large-scale productions in your chosen style. Although there is much we can learn from such productions, sometimes you can learn more from a small-scale production at a local arts centre where the equipment and space available are more comparable with what you probably have at your disposal at your school or college. Local universities and colleges can also be very useful. It's a good idea to have seen as many as three or four such productions before you embark on this project.

Sometimes you can learn a lot from a production that isn't entirely successful. What were your expectations before the performance? How could it have been better? Where exactly were the problems? What was the production trying to achieve, and where did it find difficulties? How did it fail to find a harmony between theatrical style, content and manner?

Finally, **don't put the abstract first**: let it emerge. You may have started with a fairly abstract theme, such as 'to explore naturalistically the effect of personal tragedy on a tightly-knit community', but when it comes to devising your production, you need to achieve this aim through concrete details: a real sense of community, a clear moment of tragedy, a thoughtful development and exploration of conflict and crisis. At your preview performances you should be able to evaluate whether your audience was able to distil the abstract idea – the meaning, if you like – from the concrete drama.

Developing a dramatic imagination

In order to achieve this concrete theatre from your abstract thoughts and from your research, you need to develop and practice using a more dramatic imagination.

It's easier to demonstrate this than explain it. Original drama does not have to be literal. Both research into the literal, actual world and metaphor are important, even if they lead in opposite directions to start with. The best realistic drama, such as Ibsen's and Strindberg's, uses both metonymy and metaphor. Don't be afraid to use your imaginations. Base your drama on the actual, the possible, but don't be afraid to imagine the impossible.

Rehearse the following scene. Try to notice the verbal rhythms: the rhythms within each speech and, more importantly, the rhythms created by the juxtaposition of the two voices. Think about set. Would a realistic set suit this dialogue? What would be the advantages and disadvantages of such a set? Hopefully this exercise will help you to think about dramatising the impossible, surreal or unlikely. You have to make sure, of course, that such work will end up in harmony with your chosen overall style.

Child:	You don't belong here, do you?
Man:	In a way.
Child:	In a way you do, or in a way you don't?
Man:	Well, yes, in a way, I do, and in a way I don't. [*Pause*] I was born in that house. [*Pause*]
Child:	My dad's?
Man:	Number 17.
Child:	But you don't live there any more, do you?
Man:	Maybe not.
Child:	[*Pause*] Are you grown up now? Are you a man?
Man:	I suppose I am. Though right now I'm imagining being a boy, here, in number 17.
Child:	And are you happy? I'd like to be grown up.
Man:	I was happy, I think, but I don't know for sure. Maybe I was happy. Things were good. There were no problems; we didn't have any problems. Don't think so.
Child:	What sort of problems?
Man:	I guess no one knows when they're really happy.
Child:	What sort of problems? Do all adults have problems?
Man:	I think growing up is when you start to realise you have problems. [*Pause*] Money. Children. The future is full of problems.
Child:	I don't care about the future. I don't know what the future is.
Man:	The future is the difference between you and me.

Child:	The future is birthdays and the future is holidays. The future is a snow man on the rec and fireworks.
Man:	[*Pause*] Fireworks.
Child:	What did you do when you lived here?
Man:	The future is birthdays and the future is holidays. The future is a snow man on the rec and fireworks.
Child:	[*Pause*] Fireworks.
Man:	What did you do when you lived here?
Child:	Well, I went to school.
Man:	I go to school. I walk there every morning with my mother and then in the afternoon she collects me and we walk home.
Child:	I used to walk to school. The Oriel School. A mile through the estate.
Man:	I used to walk to school. The Oriel School. A mile through the estate.
Child:	The Oriel.
Man:	If I had it all again. [*Pause*] If I had it all again, I wonder if it would all have been the same.
Child:	It will all be the same. It will all be the same again.
Man:	Will it?
Child:	I go to school. I walk there every morning with my mother and then in the afternoon she collects me and we walk home.
Man:	You don't belong here, do you?
Child:	In a way.
Man:	In a way you do, or in a way you don't? [*Pause*]
Child:	Well, yes, in a way, I do, and in a way I don't.
Man:	And what will happen next?
Child:	You know what will happen next. You know.
Man:	I know.

Shaping and structuring

A play, even a short one, must have a strong structure to be successful. Although there is a lot of instinct in the way a playwright structures a play, there's a degree of cool analysis, too. As you are working in a group, you must try to articulate your own instincts and turn them into cool analysis.

> In this instance, Lorca seems to be following the model of Greek tragedy, where the alternation between 'character' sections and chorus sections has a similar effect.

Structure is important but its forms are very subtle. In Lorca's play *Yerma* there is very little change of mood: it's all very intense and highly-charged. This is deliberate, of course, and ensures that the final climax is a terrifying resolution. However, within the play there is a carefully controlled management of scenes. Some have just one or two characters in them, making them intense and intimate; others, like the scenes with the washerwomen or the ritual dance, have many characters on stage, which changes the feel of the piece without breaking its overall direction and intensity. Analysing the structure of a piece like this will reveal, as we shall see, the nuances of its construction.

Music Composers are deeply concerned with the structures of their music. Without a verbal language to pattern their pieces with articulated themes and ideas, they must rely on repetition and development to create the emotional and intellectual effects they seek. Pay attention to the structure of some familiar (or even some unfamiliar) pieces of music. Notice how repetition is used to develop ideas; notice the use of a theme and its variations. Notice where the climaxes occur and the function of the introduction and the coda. Romantic music tends to finish like a Shakespearean play: there's a huge flourish, and we are in no doubt about the fact that the piece has concluded. Modern music, like modern drama, is a little more ambiguous: the endings seem more open.

> **Further study**
>
> Find out about sonata form in music. Can a play be written in this form? What would be the benefits?

Photos You might find it useful when shaping your piece to take digital photographs of key moments. By pinpointing these, you are shaping the piece; by photographing them, you are clarifying ideas about design and staging; by using the photographs to structure your piece, you are thinking carefully about the placing of climaxes and the overall movement of the piece. If you are the group's designer, you may find digital photographs very useful – using a computer program such as Adobe Photoshop will enable you to manipulate images to experiment with different design elements – the use of coloured lighting, for example.

Clocks In 1967, Paul McCartney and John Lennon sketched out their ideas for the Beatles' film *The Magical Mystery Tour* as a kind of wheel or clock. They divided the planned film into slices and then filled each one. Their idea was to create a balanced structure by seeing the whole as a series of complementary parts. Neil Aspinall describes this in *The Beatles Anthology* (Cassell 2000):

> Paul and John sat down in Paul's place in St John's Wood. They drew a circle, and then marked it off like the spokes on a wheel. It was a case of "We can have a song here, and a dream sequence there," and so on. They mapped it out.

Let's borrow this idea. If you study a play carefully, you will see that it is structured through a series of episodes (which may or may not be quite the same as 'scenes'). Some episodes will be fast in pace, light or humorous in tone and full of characters; others may be slow in pace, heavy, tragic or thoughtful in tone and may employ just one or two voices. You will also find that repetition is used as part of structure. In *Hamlet* there are comic and (relatively) light scenes, but the play is structured around slow, thoughtful scenes in which Hamlet is either alone or with just one or two other characters. By examining the structure of the play, we have discovered something (rather obvious, maybe) about its meaning and how this meaning is achieved. Comedies can be broken down in the same way: they tend to incorporate scenes which have a faster pace and which use a greater number of parts. But there may still be key episodes (as there are in *Twelfth Night*) where things take a more tragic turn with slow, thoughtful scenes involving just two or three characters.

When we plan our time-wheel, we should think about all this. It's a good idea to start by analysing a play in the theatrical style you've chosen, through a clock structure. You'll see then how the system works, and how your play works, too. You might be surprised by the insights provided by analysing the structure of a play in this way. Scenes whose function seemed cloudy or vague suddenly make sense: they are needed to break up the monotony of one theme or to balance a similar scene elsewhere.

> You'll probably need to annotate your time-wheel with arrows and colours to show the use of motifs and other structural material.

When you've done this, you'll be ready to work on your own scheme. You might start by deciding, for example, that as your work is going to be a thoughtful and solemn piece about a serious issue, most of your slices will be slow-paced, thoughtful and relatively solitary affairs. You might particularly want the first and last scenes to be of this serious nature. You might balance these with busier scenes and some humour. You will place the climaxes at appropriate points, which may be a little way before the end, so that there can be a final, reflective scene. And so on.

You may consider using sound to shape the mood of your piece. Now that you've made a start with your time-wheel, you could use a computer to create a collage of different kinds of music, each capturing the mood of each slice of your clock pie, with repetitions to echo repetitions in your chosen structure. If you play this during some early run-throughs, you'll be able to use sound to help establish and maintain mood and to control pace. This can be very effective.

Sound

Design factors

Designers may want to attach colours to each slice or comment about the intensity of light, so that they can consider developments and changes in mood and atmosphere.

Preparing a script

Subtext

When you are devising your script, remember the importance of subtext. In some theatrical styles, subtext is essential. In most it is important. Only in a few can it be safely ignored.

Your piece will be short in theatrical terms, so don't waste a line. It's no good just showing us breakfast. We have all seen people pass the sugar: it's not interesting. What we want to see is a breakfast where, for example, lovers are suddenly revealed to each other in the unforgiving morning light, no longer the young things of the evening before. We want to hear the anxiety and doubt in their voices, anxieties and doubts about their relationship and about the adult jealousies which are beginning to form in their minds. When a character like this asks for the sugar, we read all sorts of things into the gesture that is offered in reply, the lack of eye contact, the silence. In the subtext we hear the real relationship developing. Breakfast suddenly becomes interesting.

Uncle Vanya Let us use an extract from Chekhov's *Uncle Vanya* to demonstrate the work that actors and director can do to explore emotion through action.

> *Enter ASTROV with a map.*
>
> **Astrov:** Good afternoon.
>
> *He shakes hands with her.*
>
> You wanted to see what I've been painting?
>
> **Yelena:** You promised yesterday you'd show me your work. Can you spare the time?
>
> **Astrov:** Of course.
>
> *He spreads the map out on the card-table and fixes it with drawing pins.*
>
> Where were you born?
>
> **Yelena:** (*Helps him*) St Petersburg.
>
> **Astrov:** And where did you study?
>
> **Yelena:** At the conservatoire.
>
> **Astrov:** You may not find this very interesting.
>
> **Yelena:** Why not? I don't know the country, it's true, but I've read a lot.
>
> **Astrov:** I've got my own work-table in the house here. In Vanya's room. When I get completely exhausted, and I can't think properly any more, I drop everything and come running over here to distract myself with this thing for an hour or two. Vanya and Sonya click away on the abacus, and I sit beside them at my table, busy with my colouring, and it's warm and peaceful, and the cricket chirps. I don't allow myself this pleasure very often, though – once a month.
>
> (*Indicates the map.*)

Now, look at this. It represents this part of the country as it was 50 years ago. The light and dark green colouring indicates forest; half of the entire surface-area is forest. Where the green is hatched with red there were elk and wild goats. I've indicated the fauna as well as the flora. On this lake there were swans and geese and ducks, and what the old people call a power of birds of every sort – the place was swarming with them. Apart from the villages, look, you can see a scattering of various settlements and smallholdings, little monasteries, watermills. Cattle and horses were abundant. They're marked in blue. This district, for example, was thick with blue; there were complete herds, and two or three horses per farm.

(*Pause*) Now let's look down here. As it was 25 years ago. By this time only a third of the surface-area is under forest. The goats have gone, but there are still elk. The green and blue are paler now. And so on, and so on. Let us move on to the third section – the district as it is today. There's green here and there, but it's not solid, it's only in patches; the elk, the swans, and the capercaillies have all vanished. Of the former settlements, smallholdings, monasteries, and mills – not a trace. Overall it's the picture of a gradual but incontrovertible decline, which by the look of it will be complete in another 10 or 15 years. You'll tell me that civilizing factors are at work here, that the old life must naturally give way to the new. And, yes, I see that if these ruined forests had been replaced by roads and railways, if there were factories and schools here, then the peasants would be healthier and wealthier and wiser – but nothing of the kind!

The district still has the same swamps and mosquitoes, the same lack of roads, the same poverty and typhus and diphtheria and fires. What we are faced with here is a decline resulting from the unequal struggle for existence, a decline brought about by stagnation, by ignorance, by a total lack of awareness, by frozen, sick, and hungry men who, to preserve the last flickers of life, to save their children, instinctively, blindly, grasp at anything they can use to relieve their hunger and warm themselves, and who destroy it all without thought for the morrow. Almost everything has been destroyed now; and nothing yet has been created in its place.

(*Coldly*) I see from your face that you're not interested.

Further reading

Uncle Vanya by Anton Chekhov, translated by Michael Frayn (Methuen 1987).

Yelena:	I understand so little about it.
Astrov:	There's nothing to understand – you're simply not interested.
Yelena:	I was thinking about something else, to tell you the truth. Forgive me.

 Consider the following subtexts:

1. Astrov and Yelena are madly in love with one another but have never been able to say so.

2. Yelena loves Astrov madly but he seems oblivious to her charms.

3. Astrov finds Yelena boring but wants to use her as an intermediary in order to meet Sonya, her step daughter, with whom he is infatuated.

4. Yelena finds Astrov boring but wants to introduce him to Sonya who is infatuated with him.

5. Yelena lusts after Astrov but he is gay.

6. Everyone has told Astrov that Yelena loves him – except Yelena herself!

7. Yelena's husband is having an affair with Astrov's wife.

8. Astrov and Yelena were engaged to be married but are now happily married to others.

9. Yelena wants to ask Astrov to lend her some money but she's bored stiff by his maps!

How does each of these statements affect the way the piece is performed? How are the actions different? Work in pairs on one of each of these scenarios, and present yours to the group. Which is most convincing? Why?

If you've read *Uncle Vanya*, you'll know that some of the versions given above simply cannot be true. But an audience seeing the play for the first time may be weighing up several such possibilities.

Once you've read the scene through, you'll get the gist. Act it out without a script, improvising as accurately as you can the opening and final exchanges, and the long speech about the land-use maps. Which is the 'true' situation, do you think? Notice how by adding a subtext to our performance we are turning a lecture about Russian land-use into something a lot more interesting.

Shaping ideas as a group

You've got to work together to develop your piece: as we have noted before, cooperation and dividing up labour are key to success.

You must fight lead-actor syndrome – everyone must contribute on an equal footing – but also you must fight modesty.

Improvisation

One technique for moving from ideas to a script involves working in threes or fours on improvising dialogue. Once you have established the basic shape and function of a scene, you can begin improvising it, using your own words. Maybe two or three actors are required to play characters in the scene. A third or fourth member of the group (perhaps the designer, if you have one) simply listens, but notes down any moment, interchange, reaction or line that is really effective. After you've gone through the scene, the note-taker will report to the group and, after some discussion, you can agree to keep in some of these effective pieces. Work through the piece again, maybe this time taking different roles. The point is to allow the piece to emerge from disciplined improvisation: achieving this is key to making progress.

It may be useful here to borrow some ideas from language study. In analysing spoken language in dialogue and conversation, three forms of behaviour can be identified. Sometimes, one of the characters will be proactive, leading discussion and prompting developments and decisions; other characters will be reactive, following the lead set by the more proactive members. (You may well find your own group begins like this, before you move on to a more equitable arrangement!) Ideally, your group will represent a third stance: collaboration.

> In improvising scenes, it can be useful to identify proactive, reactive and collaborative characters. You will find that such discussions will also shed light on the relative status of the characters.

Designers

You won't all be choosing acting as your specific skill. This doesn't mean, of course, that you shouldn't all take part in preliminary improvisation sessions. In many ways, involving all the group in such sessions can be a very good strategy. However, if you are focusing on a design skill, you must make sure that as the work progresses, your design ideas are strong and individual.

Evaluating ideas

After you have spent some time preparing scenes and dialogues, you need to evaluate them. The process of devising and now the process of evaluation will give you plenty to write about in your notes.

Design

You need to ask yourselves questions about how you want the audience to react, what you want them to think about and how you want them to feel. This is the point where design ideas about costume, use of mask (if any), set, sound and lighting need to be fully integrated and discussed, whether you are focusing on this element rather than acting, or whether the design features are going to be shared around the group. Some key ideas will need to be discussed alongside the devising of the first scenes. You don't need to make firm decisions straight away – you should spend some time during each of the early sessions reviewing staging decisions: where is the piece going to be performed, on what kind of stage/set, with what costumes and sound effects?

Rationale

Do not make hasty decisions. You must have a rationale for your decisions. If you decide, as Artaud might have done, to hold your play in a barn or a hangar (this seems unlikely, but the point is clear), you must have a reason, and the reason must relate to your initial aims and objectives, too. All of this should be detailed in your notes. Even if you do not have a designated designer, do not leave decisions about set, lighting and props until the end. Make the look and sound of the play organic. Always keep your primary aim in mind.

Producing a script

At some point, even if you are working from a detailed scenario, you will have to write something down. Ideally, you will produce a script that you will work with professionally during your preparation and rehearsal sessions.

There are some key points to add here. Keep in mind that this is still an ensemble piece: make sure you work together, even if you have a talented writer in your group who takes the lead in some areas. Evaluation and analysis are important roles for everyone.

Language

Writing a play is not easy. You must understand the artificiality of theatrical language. Although you may have jotted down some phrases you've heard spoken, either during research or during improvisation sessions, a script that relies exactly on the language people use as they go about their daily business will be a very dull script. And although interruptions and unfinished utterances are natural in life, these don't always work on stage, and must be used with care.

> Phatic refers to the type of speech that expresses our sociability rather than communicating ideas or information. So, for instance, to say 'Good morning, how are you today?' or perhaps to discuss the weather is to use phatic language.

Have a look again at the extract from Chekhov's *Uncle Vanya* and at the scene between the *MAN* and *CHILD*. Note how both take the ordinary language of daily life and heighten it for the stage. Try to imagine how this conversation might actually sound in reality: more fragmentary, perhaps, with fewer grammatically correct sentences; different kinds of pauses; slang or more phatic language and so on. It can be a good idea to spend some time reading a play script – maybe just rereading a text you're studying – to remind yourselves of the special kind of artificial language which all plays use. You need to think explicitly about the tone your characters achieve, and about the tone of the play. The precise choice of language will influence pace and feel, and you may need to rework the wording to get the effect just right. This will take time and care.

It is a huge mistake to think you can improvise during your final performance. In this unit, improvisation is a tool, not a product. Improvisation will lean quite heavily towards the norms of your own expression. This is fine: but in a performance your character must have his or her own idiolect. Working on this, as playwrights from Shakespeare to Congreve and Chekhov have done, is an important part of playwriting. Scripts produced through improvisation require some editing to bring out the different flavours of the characters' voices and use of language.

Remember the old saying: 'everything is bigger on stage'. This is true of language, too. The language of all your characters will be a kind of heightened version of the real language we'd expect to meet in daily life. Look again at your set texts and see just how true this is.

Preparing a performance

Actioning the text

When Stanislavski worked on Chekhov's plays, notably *Three Sisters* and *The Cherry Orchard*, he constantly wrote to Chekhov, then living in the Crimea, to ask for advice and explanation regarding the text. Obviously this is not always possible. In his book *Letters to George* (Nick Hern Books 1997), director Max Stafford-Clark explains how he too is used to dealing with contemporary playwrights in this manner. But he goes on to detail the rehearsals for a production of a Restoration play by George Farquhar, who had been dead for over 200 years and therefore was not able to reply to letters nor answer the phone. Stafford-Clark's solution to this was to write down a report of each day's work as a letter to the playwright, sharing anxieties, articulating problems, and praising effective and successful scenes.

In other words, *Letters to George* is a giant example of your working notes. At this stage of the preparation process, you too could write letters or diary entries reporting on progress. Of course, as one of the devisers of the piece, you should be able to answer some of the problems or question how things have developed. All of this is very valuable.

In *Letters to George*, Stafford-Clark outlines a brilliant rehearsal technique based on actioning the text. Firstly, he starts his rehearsals with a script, with the actors sitting around a table (remember that he's already asked them to undertake key research activities to inform their understanding of the play and of their roles within it). The focus is on the text and breaking it down to understand what is behind what the characters say. That's one reason why it is so important, after all your experimentation, improvisation, writing and editing, to produce a polished, written script.

Actioning

The idea behind Stafford-Clark's actioning technique is this: when people speak, especially in a play, it is not idle chatter, or saying words merely for the sake of saying them. There is some motivation behind them. This motivation provides a context for what they have said. (Analysis of spoken language along these lines is called 'pragmatics'.) For instance, they may be threatening someone, warning someone, or flirting with someone – they are performing some action through speaking. Stafford-Clark argues that a key role of rehearsal is to establish just what action each speech – or each section of a longer speech – is fulfilling. He and his cast would take each speech, or section of speech, and decide what it is doing, what its purpose in the play is. After discussing this, they would agree on a transitive verb that they think explains what this action is; for example, to threaten, to warn, or to detain.

> Examples of transitive verbs can be found in italics in the following sentence: 'The mother *detains* her son. He *ignores* her.' A transitive verb always has an object: you cannot say 'The mother detains', you have to say who or what she detains, because the action is not one she can do on her own.

By discussing each speech in this way with the group, you will soon find how collaborative a process this is. You will also find that it should become much easier to act the play out afterwards. You focus on the underlying and agreed action of the speech as you deliver it. This will affect, for example, the pace and tone of your voice, your gestures and your body language. Since the action is represented by a transitive verb and therefore shows the effect of the speech on others, it will also influence where you put yourself on stage and how you react to the other characters. In Stanislavski's terms, it will affect the size of your circle of attention. It will also affect your relationship with the audience; after all, in some Restoration dramas, the action of a lot of the speeches is to inform the audience.

> **Further reading**
> See *Blood Wedding*, translated by Michael Dewell and Carmen Zapata in *The House of Bernarda Alba and Other Plays* by Federico García Lorca (Penguin 2001).

Devising actions to accompany text requires an understanding of what is really going on. In *Blood Wedding* by Lorca, the Mother's opening lines, are, on the face of it, pretty meaningless; what she really wants is simply to hold her son in conversation to delay his departure because she is protective of him. On the other hand, he hesitates because he wants to bring up the question of his marriage. There is more to this than a simple departure for work. Consider the following interpretation.

BRIDEGROOM: *[entering]* Mother? Why does a grown man tell his mother that he is leaving for work? Why does he need to attract her attention? Does he really want to talk about his plans for marriage? There are many interpretations. The beauty of the 'actioning' technique is that the cast clarifies its view and maintains a consistent interpretation of events.	Maybe the bridegroom does want to talk about his marriage, as becomes a little clearer later in the scene, so is testing the water with this word. Very tentative.	The bridegroom **tests** his mother.
MOTHER: Yes.	One word. But look more closely. Is the mother asking her son what he wants? Is she exasperated with him? Does she know what's coming – the question of marriage? Is she resisting this? (You'll notice how important it is for this kind of analysis that the cast knows the entire script and has a feel for the overall aims and objectives of the text.)	The mother **resists** her son. Try this in performance. Say the one word, 'Yes', in a way which resists the person who has just addressed you.

BRIDEGROOM: I'm going.	It sounds as if he's chickened out. We can all see he's going. Has he paused before his answer? Does this indeed confirm our feelings that in the first instance he was testing his mother out to see what sort of mood she was in, and whether now was a good time to talk about his fiancée? In which case this is a bit of a climb-down.	The bridegroom **subordinates** himself to his mother.
MOTHER: Where?	She knows. He works on the land; he's just bought a vineyard. Obviously that's where he's going (you would know this, having thoroughly read and researched the text before the exercise). So she's not asking a question. She's challenging him, to come out with his wedding news perhaps.	The mother **challenges** the bridegroom.
BRIDEGROOM: To the vineyard. *[He starts to go.]*	Complete surrender. He's off, without having talked about his life.	The bridegroom **surrenders** to his mother.
MOTHER: Wait.	Why? They're definitely skirting this issue, aren't they? Perhaps the mother is delaying her son to protect him (from the future) or so that they can talk about the wedding (which is what happens).	The mother **invites** her son (to continue).
BRIDEGROOM: Do you need something?	This could be aggressive or kind, on the face of it. But maybe he is frustrated with the way the mother is playing with his emotions. He could sound quite exasperated? Maybe he now is taking the upper hand, challenging his mother to talk about the future? Maybe he is challenging her; maybe he is rejecting her.	The bridegroom **challenges** his mother.

There are many ways of rehearsing a script, but finding actions to accompany the text can be an important start to the process of converting script to performance. You will need a good vocabulary, so having a thesaurus to hand is a good idea. You could just glue your script into your notes, and work on it there, producing a table like this, so that your notes directly record the discussions of the group and your final decisions.

Rehearsal techniques

Rehearsing not devising Once you've begun rehearsals, you are no longer devising – you are rehearsing. You may find you need to make slight changes to the script to match other performance issues, but these should be few and minor. If you get to the designated rehearsal period and you're still devising, you've got a problem! Sometimes, it can be best to pretend at this stage that you are actually preparing a production of someone else's play. That way, you focus on production issues and rehearsal techniques, and leave behind for good the questions of devising and structuring.

Design You are working as a team. Design ideas must be integrated with rehearsals. If you are focusing on a design element for this unit you must not work in isolation; nor should you go off and bring back your work two days before the dress rehearsal. As a team you should set out a carefully considered calendar of deadlines, so that lighting plots, soundscapes, costume, set, props and so on are prepared as they are needed, and are tested in rehearsal conditions.

Directing For all the students, as we have said, the relationship between the original piece and the chosen theatrical style is important and must be explicitly addressed somewhere in the supporting notes. However, for the director, such a link is paramount. The director is responsible for the 'communication of meaning for the audience' and that overall and essential aim must be realised through a range of strategies including:

➤ The choice and deployment of the acting space and the consequent relationship between actor and audience

➤ The interpretation of material from the single line to the whole

➤ The actions, movement, interactions and 'blocking' of the actors

➤ The creation of pace, tempo, rhythm and climax

➤ Clarifying for the actors the intentions of the piece and its success as drama.

The director has an important role in a production like this, but students must not surrender all decisions; you must work as a team. Take it in turns to stand back from performing to look at the effect of your work and to concentrate on individual scenes as they are being rehearsed. Don't look in the first place for solutions: try to identify problems. If something doesn't feel right, then it probably isn't. The director should identify moments when something doesn't feel right, but it's best if the team discusses the issue and comes up with one or more solutions to try out. This in turn provides more grist for your notes.

When you're acting as a director, resist the temptation to interrupt a scene. This can ruin the concentration of the performers and can disrupt the rehearsal so much that you never actually get to the end of the scene. The best practice is to give notes: jot down good things and problems as the scene is rehearsed, and then go through these notes quickly at the end, for whole-group discussion. Take this role in turns. It's your job as a team to respond to the comments. Don't be frightened of adverse remarks: they are really what you need. If there are problems, you need to be aware of them so they can be solved.

It is very important to aim to perform your final, examined piece without prompts at any time. But problems can arise, so make sure you have strategies in place to keep going. Identify any tricky areas and make sure you know how you can help one another on stage.

And finally, don't neglect the benefits of studying a practitioner. The work you have done on practitioners such as Stanislavski, Artaud and Craig should help you with a range of rehearsal skills and ideas. Don't partition your course so that your units are separate, discrete areas that do not inform one another. Your practical performance should, in some key ways, represent a synopsis of all you have learned in your A-level course.

Performance preparation

As the day of the examined performance approaches, you will feel increasingly anxious. This is a good thing. But you must adopt the kind of behaviour which will not exacerbate the tension.

Be organised

Keep your space tidy. It's amazing how frustrating it is to rehearse in a space where the cast have abandoned their bags and coats all over the place as they have arrived. It's maddening when props are moved or carelessly discarded. Keep unnecessary stuff out of the theatre, and be orderly and cooperative about the props you require.

Punctuality is essential during the whole unit, naturally, but now it is paramount. Everyone will be on edge, so a five-minute delay when one member of the cast turns up late for a rehearsal can produce huge anxiety and ruin the value of the session. You may be sharing a space with another group: this is another reason for tidiness and punctilious time-keeping. Turn up well organised and in good time.

Relationships

You will be very stressed, so make an effort to adopt quite formal manners. It's amazing how a little casual comment can provoke friction at this stage! By adopting careful spoken manners and by thinking first before speaking, a lot of stress can be dissipated. This may sound old-fashioned, but it's excellent advice. Being polite can help you to avoid communicating your own anxieties.

You are working together. Everyone knows about the acting profession's 'luvvie' culture – don't be ashamed of this. When you're feeling anxious or nervous, it can be really helpful if a friend and colleague tells you how well you're doing. Go out of your way to praise your partners. Help one another to feel good about what you are doing and you will all do it better.

Atmosphere Try to create an ambience in your performance space so that you find it easy to establish the mood of your piece. Consider background music as you (and later, the audience) arrive; think about the exact quality of the house lighting as you undertake those final rehearsals. You may not want a battery of strip lights, even when you are not using your final lighting plot. Ambience in these final sessions can be very helpful.

The notes Put aside time for completing your notes. Don't mix rehearsal time with notes time. Your notes are now almost entirely a personal and independent task: work on them on your own. Don't irritate others by claiming rehearsal time for yourself!

Finally, when it comes to the performance itself, the key thing is concentration. Remembering all that you have worked for and trying to help one another are essential elements of a successful performance. So are appropriate levels of performance energy and a tight focus. Prepare for all this by having a good night's sleep, arriving in plenty of time and drinking plenty of water. You should then be able to give your best – do not rely on luck.

Glossary

Comedy of manners. A comedy of manners mocks the social values of the audience viewing the play in a humorous, light-hearted way. Such comedies invite audiences to laugh at themselves, without suggesting that revolutionary change is required. In this sense, most comedies of manners are reactionary.

Commedia dell'arte. Commedia dell'arte was a dramatic form of the late Italian Renaissance which came to influence theatre throughout Europe. Actors used masks to represent their characters which led to an exaggerated, physical style of acting. Commedia plays were largely improvised in public places, and their plots involved a group of stock characters, which might include, for instance, the beautiful young woman Columbina or the greedy merchant Pantalone. Wit, topicality and physical humour were all important elements of the Commedia.

Directorial aims. Each production of a play reinterprets the text in a new way. The director working with the text, and sometimes the actors in experimental rehearsals, establish their aims for the new production; these directorial aims encapsulate the new interpretation the play undergoes.

Farce. Farce is a form of comedy whose prime purpose is to raise laughter. Its basic elements include exaggerated action, ludicrous occurrences and coincidences, slapstick and physical humour, and the depiction of larger-than-life characters. Plot and situation dominate.

Jacobean tragedy. The early 17th century (the Jacobean period of King James I) was a rich period in literary history; during this time, tragedy became violent and dark. There is little redemption in tragedies by Jacobean dramatists such as Tourneur, Middleton and Webster.

Melodrama. Melodrama was developed in England in the 19th century as a means of subverting the strict state control of theatres. By miming to music, companies were able to describe their performances as 'musical' rather than 'dramatic'. In due course, although the use of music remained important, a popular, sentimental form of drama emerged. Some melodramas dramatised sensational real-life crimes, which enabled the presentation of extremes of evil and innocence. Others began with the realistic depiction of a social problem followed by a personal problem. The personal problem was often resolved at the end, providing a happy ending in one sense, while leaving the social problem unresolved. In this way, many melodramas were reactionary in tone and effect.

Metaphor and metonymy. Expressionist writers of the early 20th century articulated extreme emotions through symbols and metaphors. Sometimes these were surreal, recalling dream imagery and the art of the surrealists. The traditional method of representation is metonymy, whereby we are shown part of the whole from which we infer the rest (for instance, we might see part of a room and infer the remainder).

The preference for metaphor over metonymy was characteristic of the modernist movement; modernists might argue that while metonymy shows what something looks like, metaphor reveals what it is.

Motif. In a usage borrowed from the analysis of music, motif is used to describe a repeated feature or gesture in a play, the repetition of which serves both as a structural device and as a clue to underlying themes.

Naturalism. Naturalism was a school of thinking that was derived from Charles Darwin's work in biology. Naturalist writers, such as Émile Zola in France, Henrik Ibsen in Norway and Thomas Hardy in England, followed Darwin's view that people (or species) were created through a combination of heredity and environment. Their writings placed emphasis on parentage and location when exploring character and motive.

Naturalist plays usually present a tense situation, whereby one small external intervention strains things to breaking point. They describe a situation, an intervention, the resulting tension, breaking point and aftermath. Realism is used to emphasise the naturalist themes, and intimate scenes are presented in realistic settings, as if the 'fourth wall' of a room has been peeled away allowing the audience to peer in.

Objective. In Stanislavski's analysis of acting, defining the objective of each character within each scene or episode is a key technique to understand motivation and purpose. (See also superobjective.)

Realism. During the 19th century, a greater emphasis was placed on realism in theatre – that is, making things look and sound as they do in real life. Many theatre companies spent enormous amounts of time and money creating the realistic appearance of a play's setting.

Restoration comedy. Following the restoration of the monarchy in England with the coronation of Charles II in 1661, the theatres reopened with renewed energy and flamboyance. The dominant theatrical form was the comedy of manners (see above). Plays were witty and scandalous, and made much of the contrast between the amoral behaviour of the city and 'backward' traditions of the country. During this period female actors became established on the English stage.

Setting. This should not be confused with the set. A play's setting refers to the imagined place and time in which it is located. Establishing a coherent setting is an important stage in defining coherent directorial aims and objectives.

Superobjective. In Stanislavski's analysis of acting, a superobjective refers to the overriding desire of a character which informs their behaviour throughout the play. Sometimes this is directly articulated by the character themselves, whereas at other times, it has to be inferred from the text.

Symbolism. Symbolism was particularly popular at the turn of the 19th century and the beginning of the 20th. Playwrights such as Yeats and Strindberg used vivid metaphors to communicate meanings which in themselves could be as difficult to articulate as the meanings contained in music or abstract art.

Index

A

aftermath 18, 63
Alexandrines 30
Artaud 76-78, 100-101, 110, 115

B

Boal 68-69
breaking point 18, 63
Brecht 42, 64-69, 80, 83, 87
breeches roles 38
Brook 64, 80, 87

C

chorus 8, 15, 60, 70, 74, 78
comedie-francaise 30
Comedy of manners 52
commedia dell'arte 17, 30, 33-34, 37, 43-44, 47
communion 54
conceptual structure 23
concrete performance 23
creative overview 29, 37, 42, 47, 51, 57

D

deus ex machina 20, 34
dialectic 66, 68
didactic 65-66
directorial aim 58-59, 62-63, 69, 73, 78, 83, 86, 89
duende 62-63

E

Elizabethan theatre 9
epic theatre 65-66, 87-88, 90

F

farce 53
fate 60-61, 71, 73
Forum Theatre 68

G

gestic acting 66
Grotowski 80, 83, 88-89

I

imagery 16, 18, 64, 75, 83
improvisation 33, 81, 97, 109-111

J

Jacobean theatre 15, 17, 24-26, 29

K

key moments 24, 26, 35, 41, 44, 49, 54, 104

L

lazzi 34

M

melodrama 12, 20, 53-56, 85-88
metaphor 18, 49, 54, 75, 78, 101
metonymy 18, 49, 63, 75, 78, 101
minimalism 67
modal verbs 23
modernist 18, 75
motivation 25, 50, 80, 111

N

naïve style 64
naturalism 18, 50, 63, 70, 72-73, 90
nihilism 75

O

objectives 39, 48, 83, 93-98, 110, 112
outsider theatre 34

P

poetry 52, 60-64
poor theatre 88-89

R

realism 13, 17-18, 48, 50-51, 61, 63, 67, 70, 72, 78, 80-81, 87, 99
received pronunciation 82
register 33, 44-45, 83, 94
Restoration comedies 17, 38, 41-42, 112
rough theatre 87

S

Seneca 25
Stanislavski 18, 39, 48-51, 54, 61, 63, 72, 77, 111-112, 115
subtext 20-21, 48, 105-106, 108
symbolism 18, 21, 29, 61, 69-70

T

text analysis
    character 10, 14, 17-18, 75-76, 78, 80-82
    costumes 9, 17, 24, 28, 44, 48, 78
    set 12, 14, 16-17, 26, 34, 50, 64, 67, 70-72, 76, 78, 80
Theatre of the Oppressed 68
total theatre 76
tragedy
    classical tragedy 60, 71-72

V

Verfremdungseffekt 66

Z

zanni 44